D0580627

BLACK OPS
BRICKS

BRICKS

HOW TO BUILD YOUR OWN MODEL MILITARY AND ARMORED FIGHTING VEHICLES

NICK GRANT

Skyhorse Publishing

Copyright © 2014 by Nicholas Grant

All rights reserved. No part of this book may be reproduced in
any manner without the express written consent of the publisher,
except in the case of brief excerpts in critical reviews or articles.
All inquiries should be addressed to Skyhorse Publishing,
307 West 36th Street, 11th Floor, New York, NY 10018.

Skyhorse Publishing books may be purchased in bulk at special
discounts for sales promotion, corporate gifts, fund-raising, or
educational purposes. Special editions can also be created to
specifications. For details, contact the Special Sales Department,
Skyhorse Publishing, 307 West 36th Street, 11th Floor, New York,
NY 10018 or info@skyhorsepublishing.com.

Skyhorse® and Skyhorse Publishing® are registered trademarks
of Skyhorse Publishing, Inc.®, a Delaware corporation.

Visit our website at www.skyhorsepublishing.com.

10 9 8 7 6 5 4 3 2 1

Library of Congress Cataloging-in-Publication Data
is available on file.

Cover design by Brian Peterson

Print ISBN: 978-1-62914-763-5
Ebook ISBN: 978-1-62914-875-5

Printed in China

Dedicated
to the
dedicated.

INTRODUCTION FROM THE AUTHOR

>> LEGO bricks are designed to inspire. They are meant to kindle the imagination and bring out the unique side of everyone. Whether that's the architect, the set designer, the maniacal genius, or the conquering hero, LEGO bricks give us the ability to be an imaginative inventor of wonderful creations. But, everyone has a different definition of wonderful. Some will build armies that will go forth and conquer all of space, even if the galaxy only stretches from the foot of the bed to the window sill. Some will create a land of fairy tales filled with technicolor vehicles that ride on mismatched tires and planes that couldn't possibly fly in our non-brick world. Then there are those who are always looking to build a better army, to have limitless LEGO power at their disposal. They continue to amass a collection of bigger, better, and faster vehicles, building each one with pride and ingenuity and discovering new techniques and better designs along the way. This book is for those vehicle maniacs. Inside you will find crazy techniques, advanced builds, and kindling for the imagination. This book gives you the structure and instructions to build the collection of amazing machines on the following pages that range from a VTOL jet, to an armored transport, and even a rotating mobile missile battery.

>> Black Ops missions encompass more than just the vehicles that cause mass destruction, it's also about the support vehicles, the day to day transports to get VIP's and criminals from point A to point B, and the impenetrable off-road mobile medical unit that just might be the key to survival for your minifig in his most dire hour. Specialized missions

aren't only about the attack helicopter that will take out anything in its path, they're also about that support helicopter that will show up with reinforcements and covering fire to save your butt in the middle of heated LEGO warfare. While there are full instructions for each vehicle in here, the idea is not to build them all and claim victory because you're finished. You're never *finished* with LEGO, there is always something new to build. If you build just one or build them all, the hope is that you'll come away with ideas for your next ten, twenty, or hundred creations. Whether that idea is as small as a new seat design that you'll put in your own next-gen fighter jet or as vast as finding a particular style of weapon that you hope to implement across your entire lego arsenal, as long as you're inspired, the idea is what counts.

Ready to get building?
Nick Grant

Play well...

L.P.V.

PAGE # 17

Swallow-tail Attack Helicopter

PAGE # 27

Snubnose Off-Roader

PAGE# **65**

Desert Recon Vehicle

PAGE# **87**

CONTENTS **13**

Armored Transport

PAGE # 101

PAGE # 135

Backup Helicopter

14

Mobile Missle Battery

PAGE #
179

PAGE #
203

VTOL Fighter Jet

CONTENTS **15**

L.P.V.
(LOCAL PATROL VEHICLE)

PIECE COUNT:
- 95 elements

FEATURES:
- Inset tires reduce overall width for transport
- Dual mounted guns

Sentry vehicle which is usually deployed from larger carrier-type vehicles to help establish a perimeter. Also deployed on bases for guard duty.

Limited range, variety of ammunition for the guns, and good turning radius.

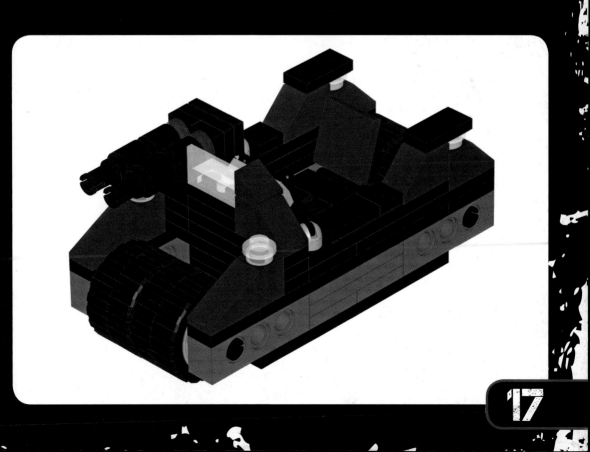

1

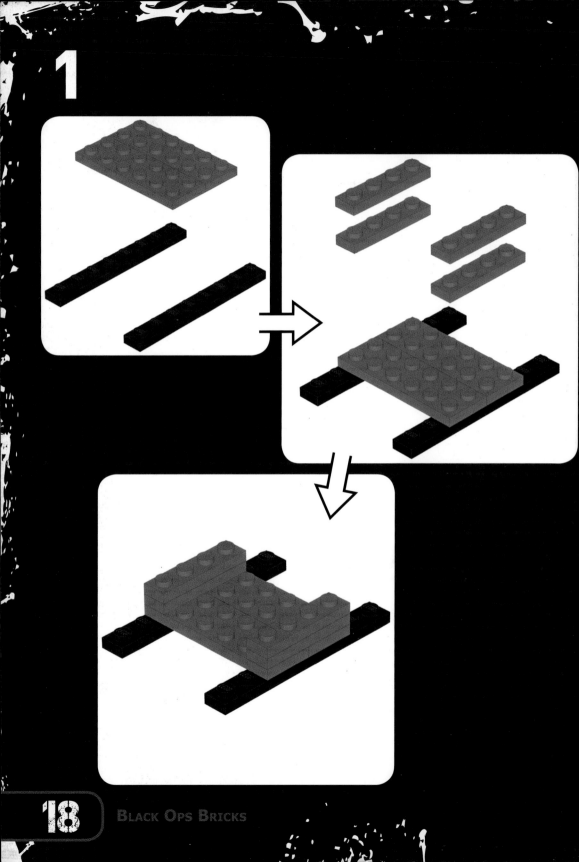

BLACK OPS BRICKS

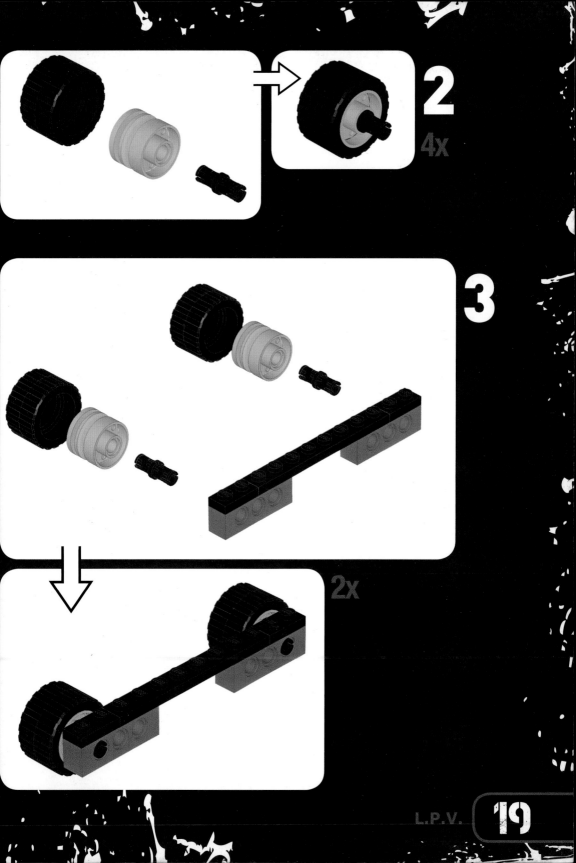

2
4x

3
2x

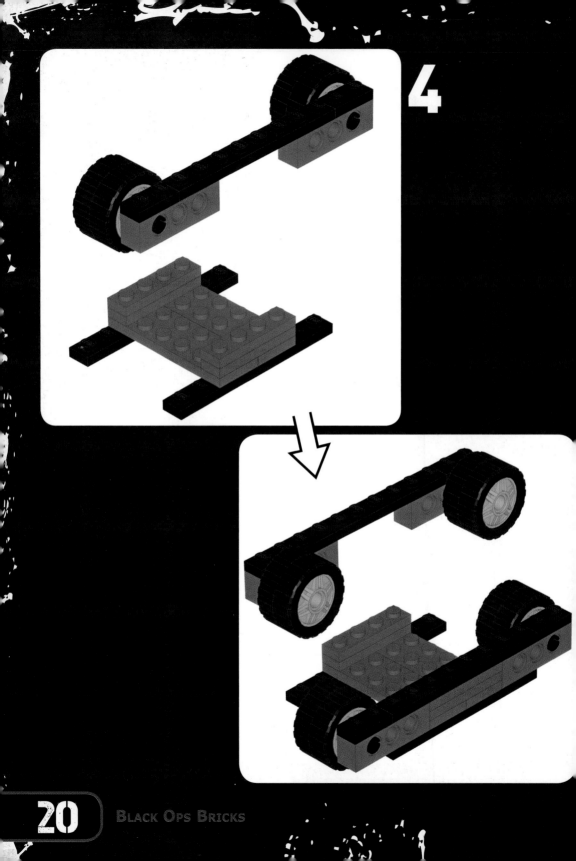

4

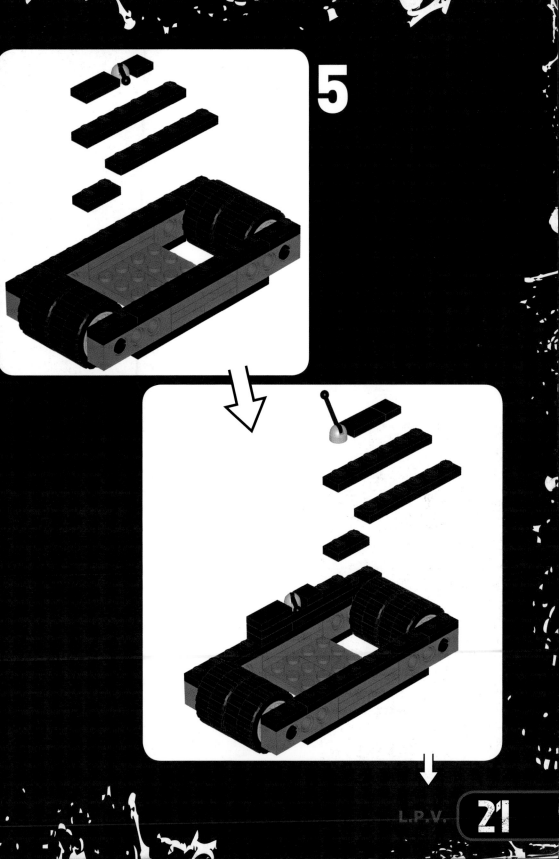

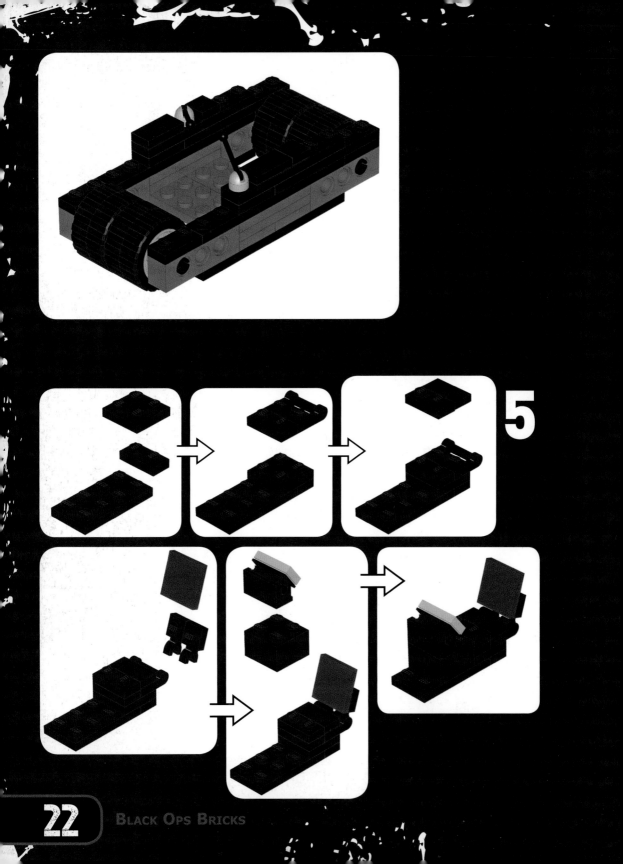

5

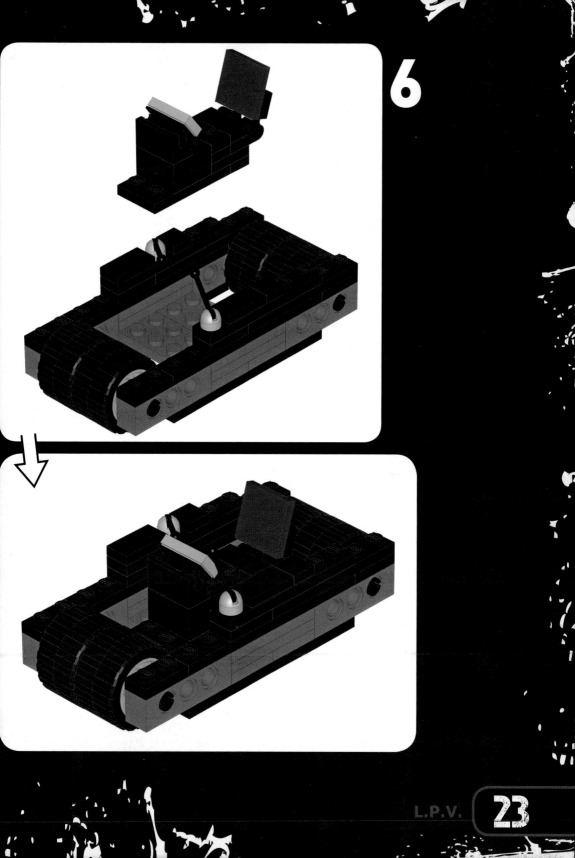

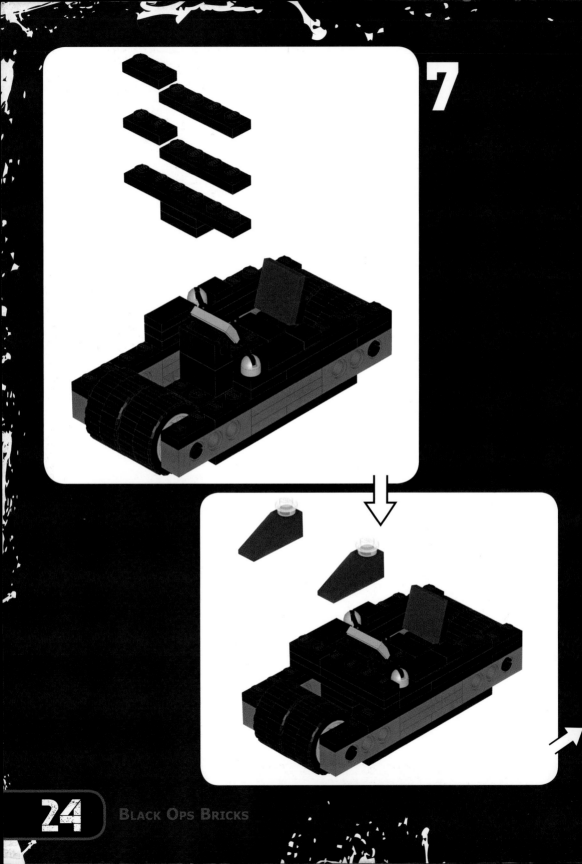

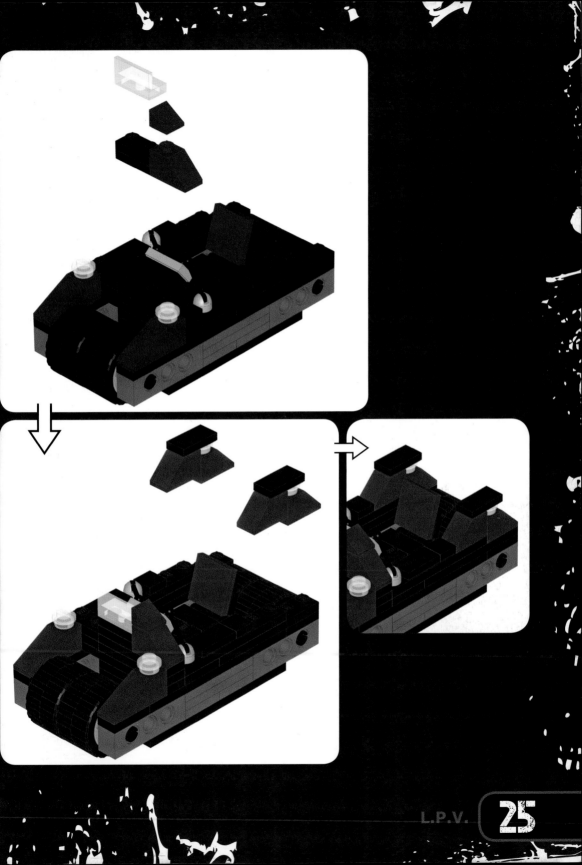

8

Done

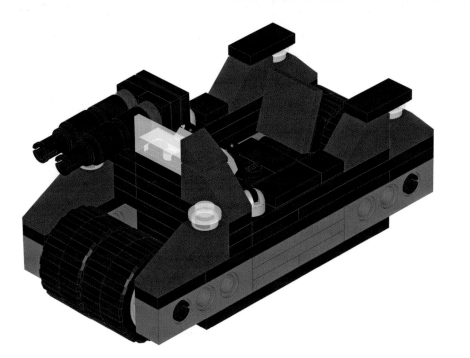

SWALLOW-TAIL ATTACK HELICOPTER

PIECE COUNT:
- 631 elements

FEATURES:
- Two pilots
- A lot of firepower
- Split tail for enhanced in-air maneuverability

Loosely based on (but greatly improves upon) the popular Cobra attack helicopter, with its big missile pods and numerous rockets.

This thing has enough firepower to keep anyone back, but the missle racks can be retrofitted for more civilian work.

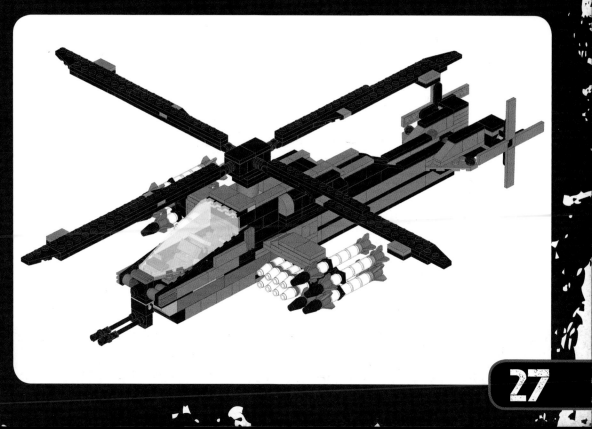

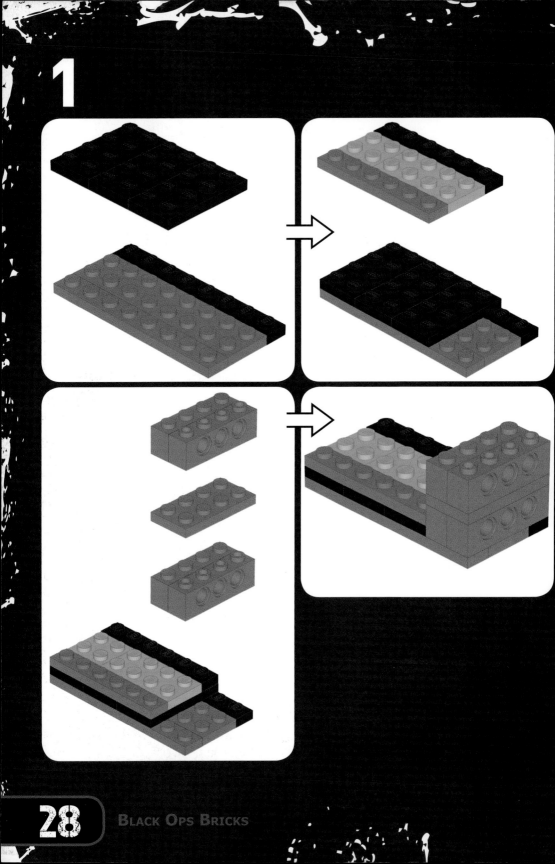

2

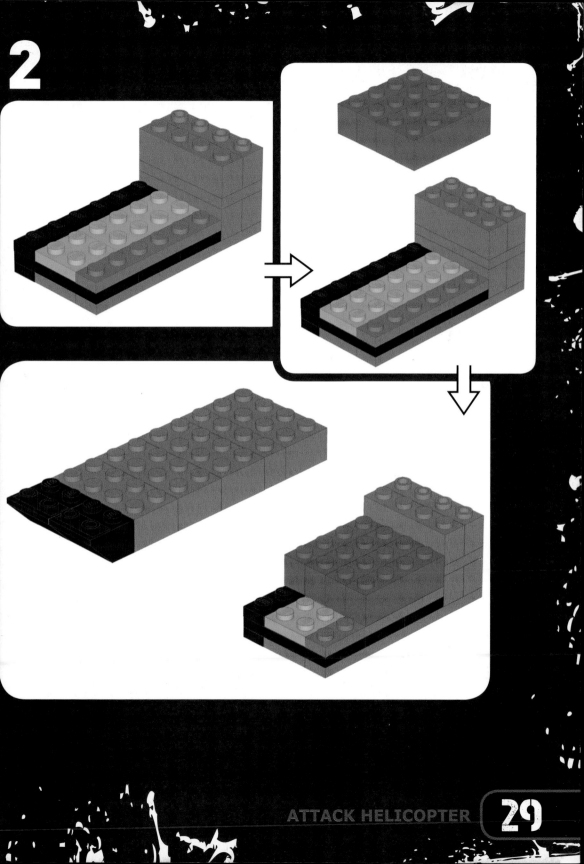

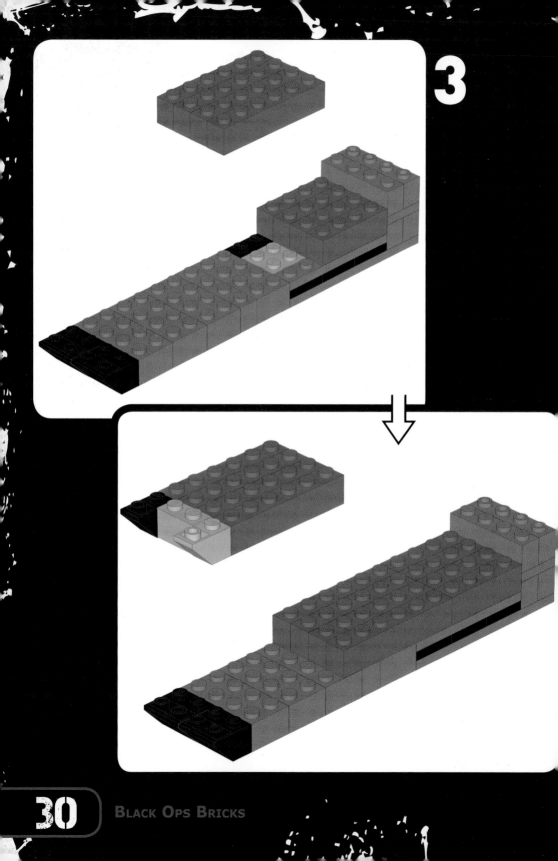

BLACK OPS BRICKS

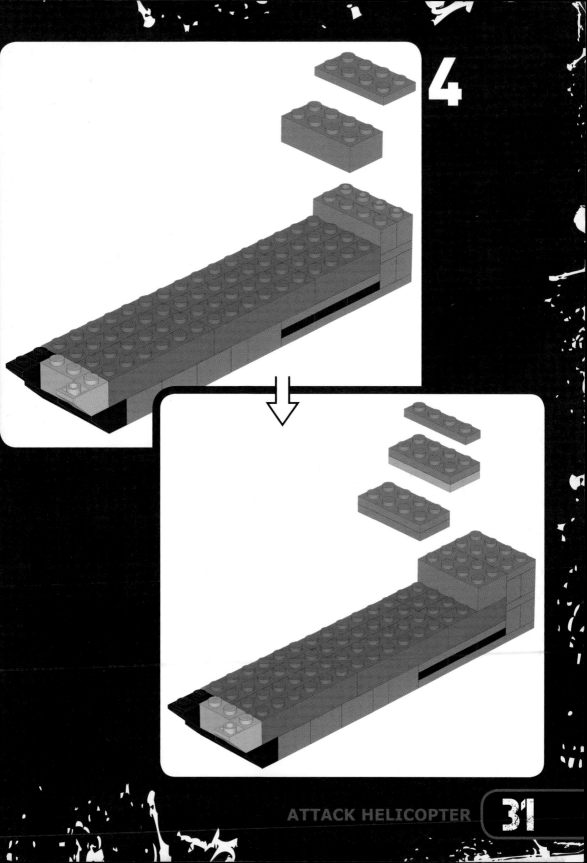

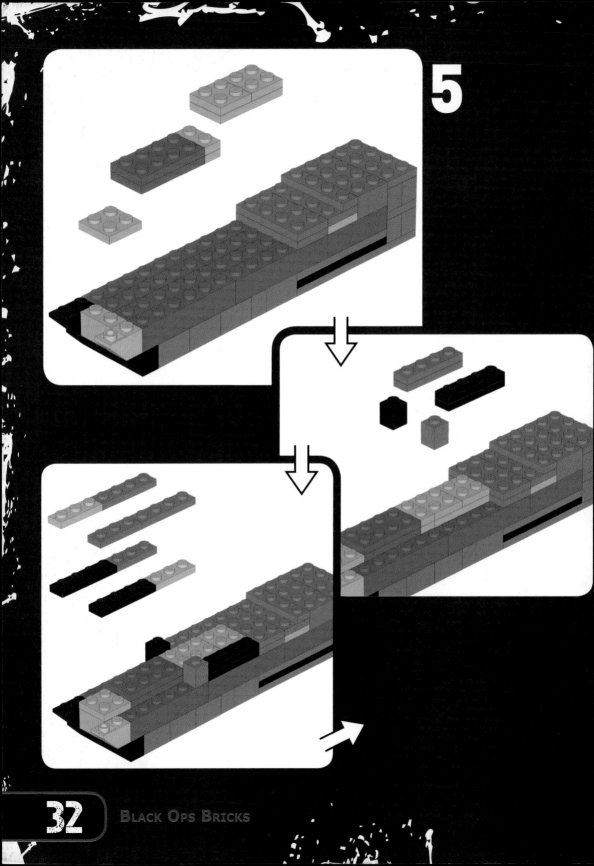

5

BLACK OPS BRICKS

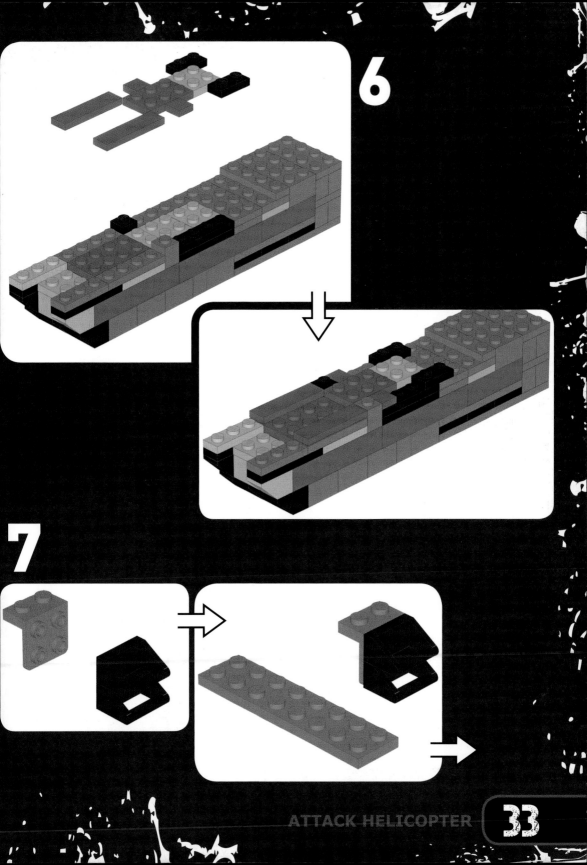

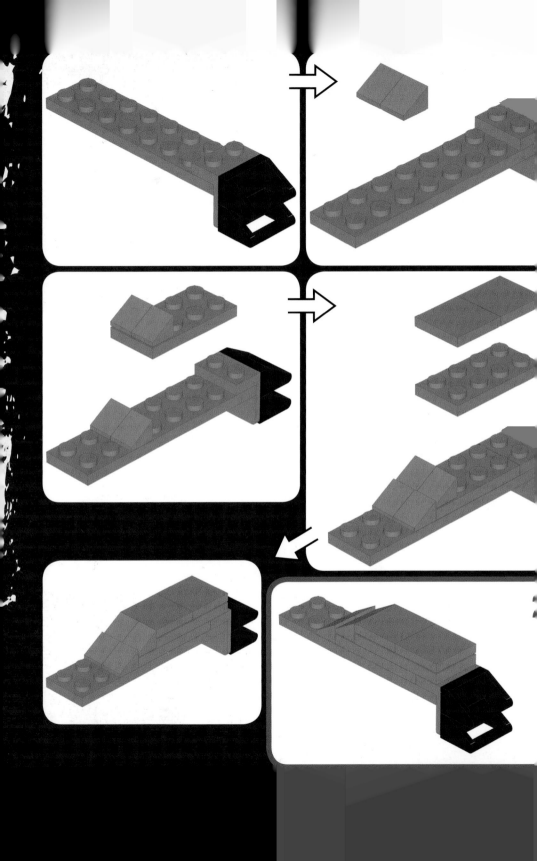

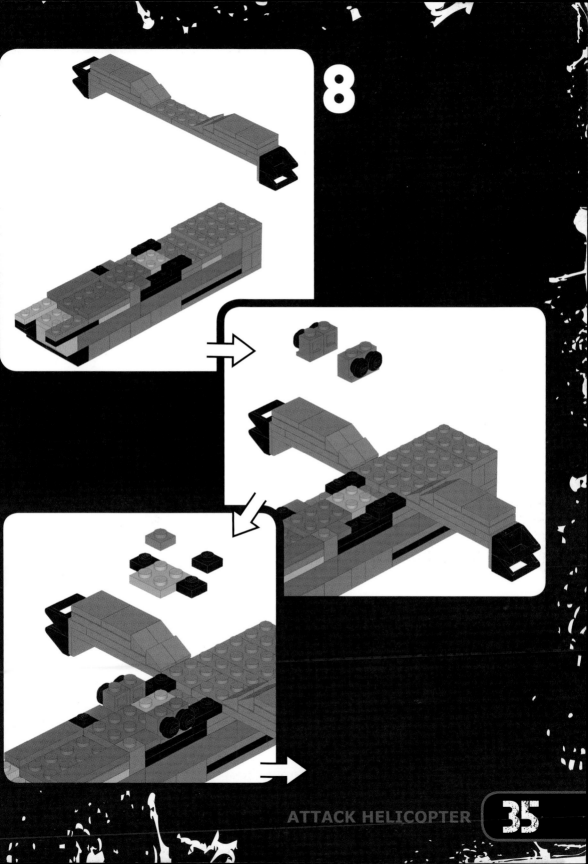

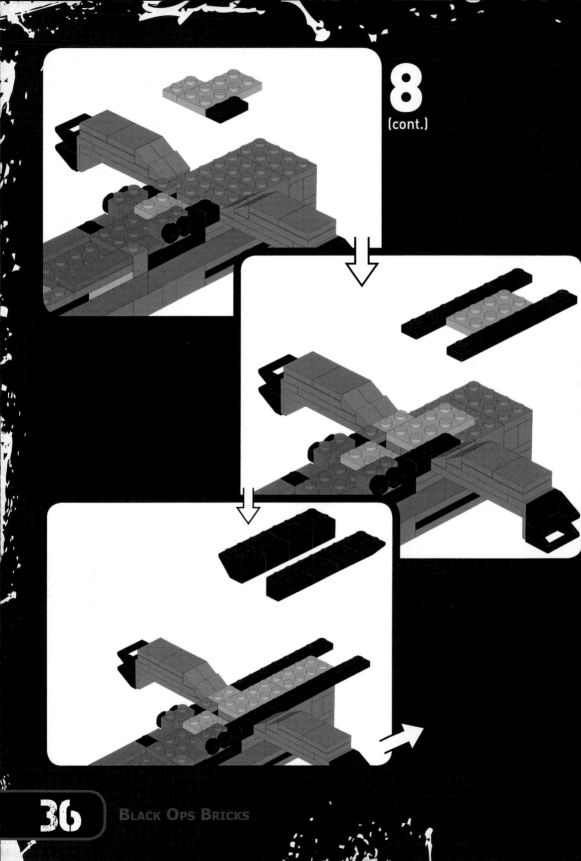

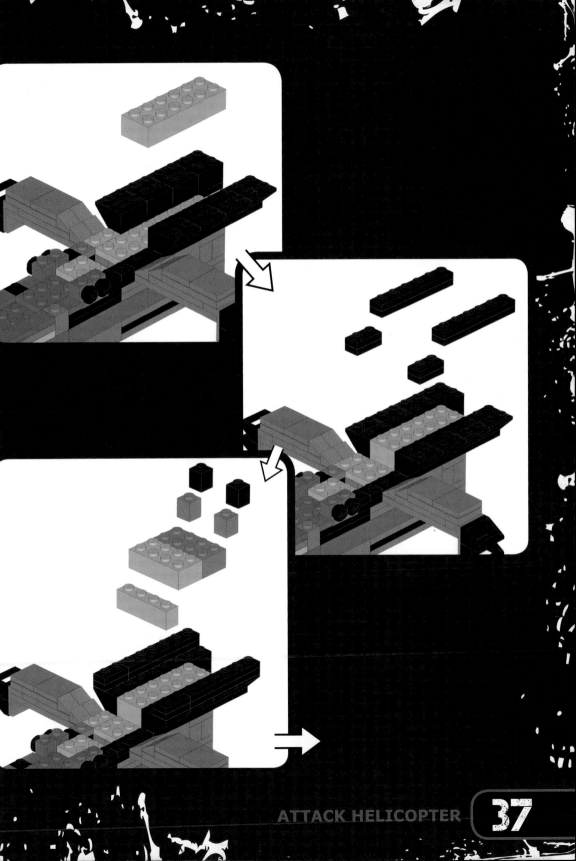

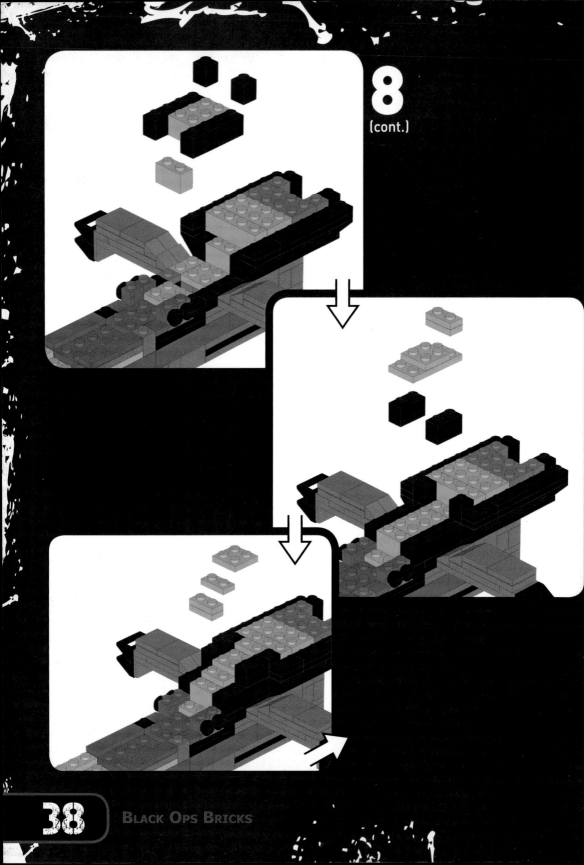

BLACK OPS BRICKS

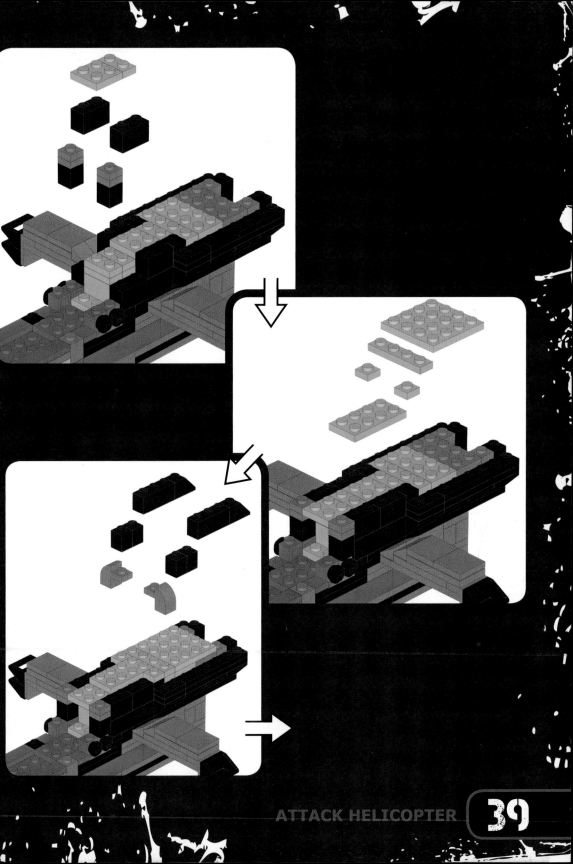

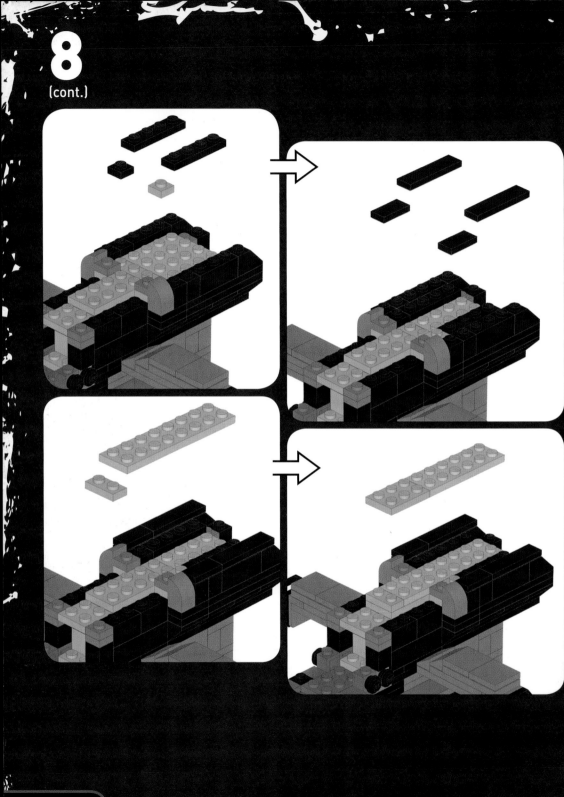

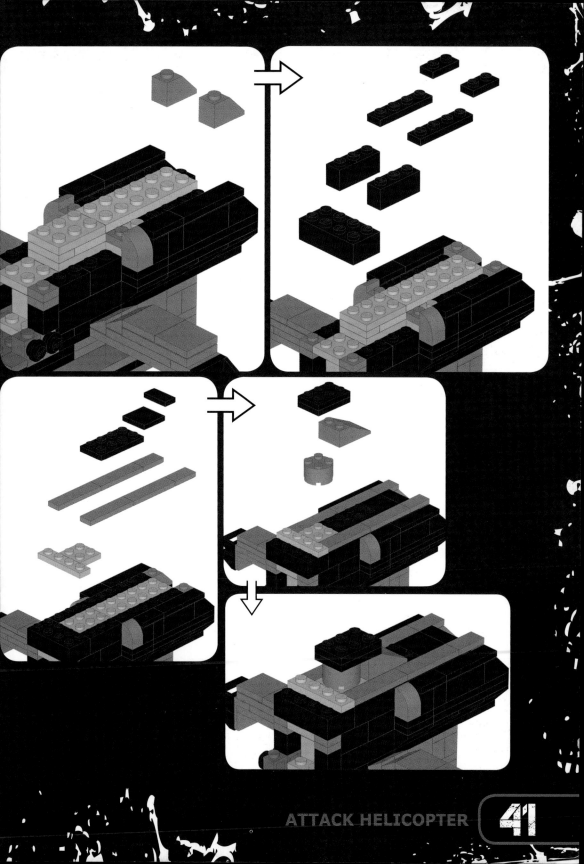

9

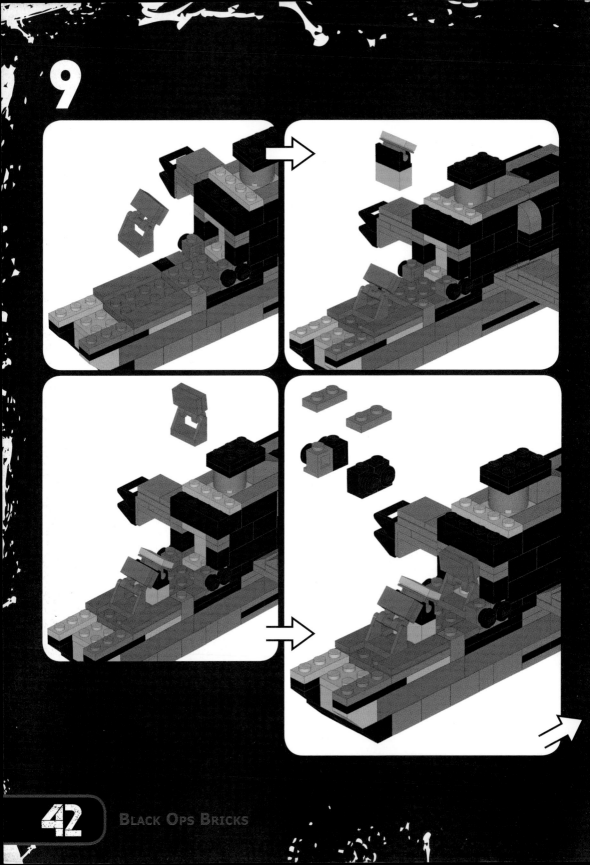

BLACK OPS BRICKS

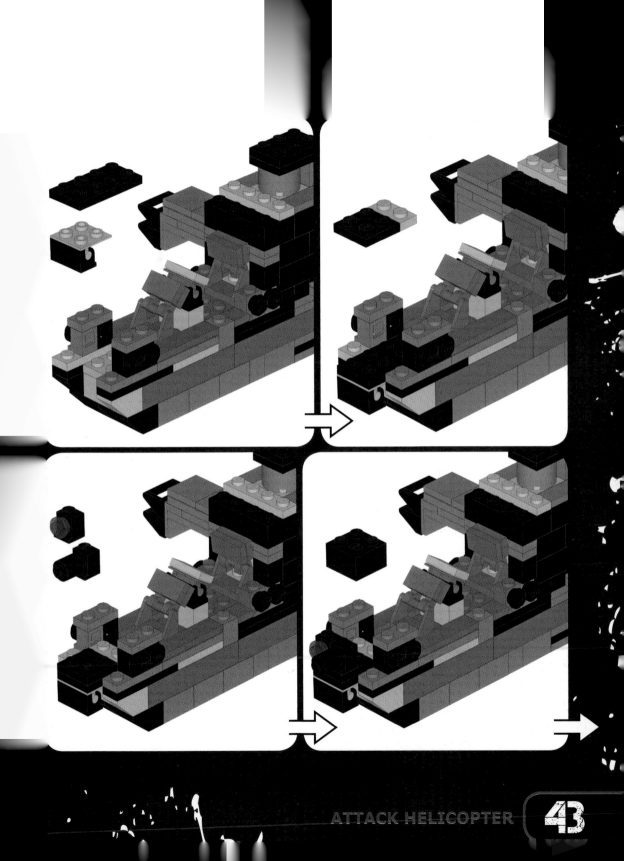

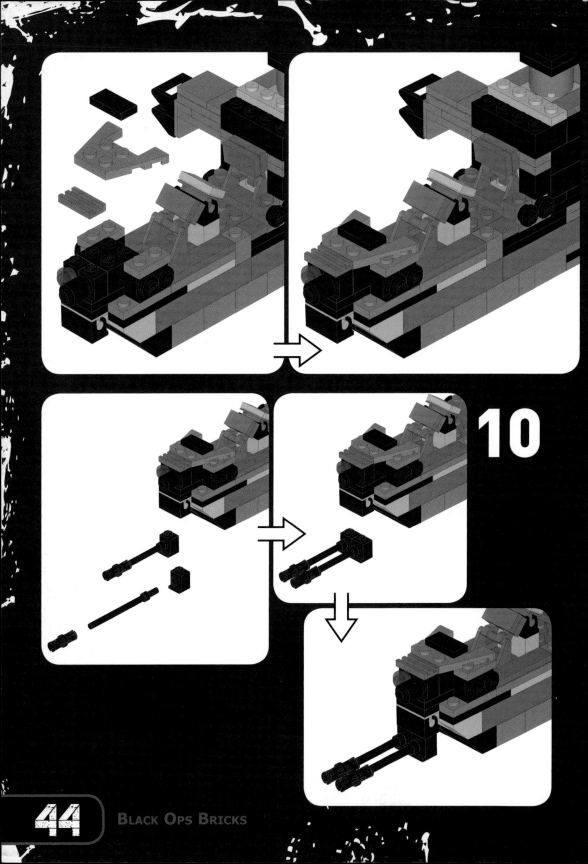

10

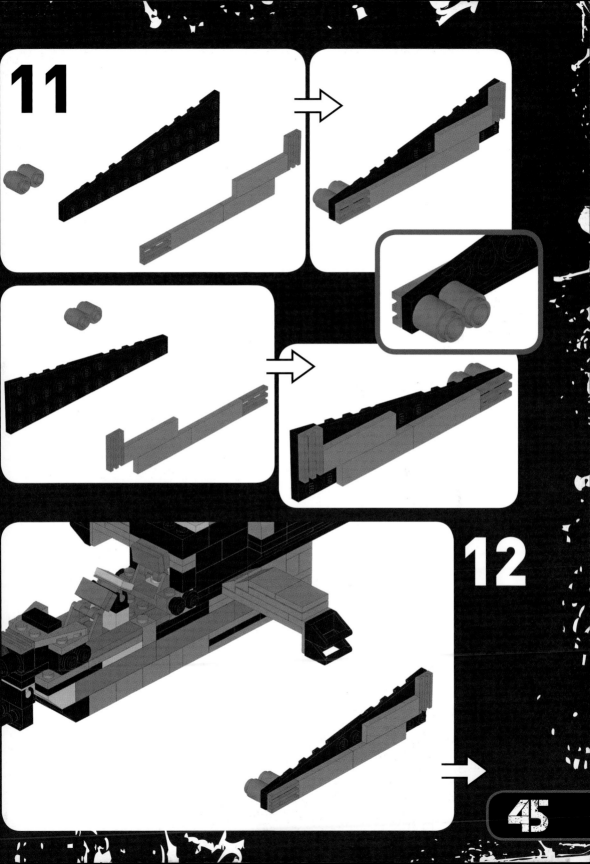

11

12

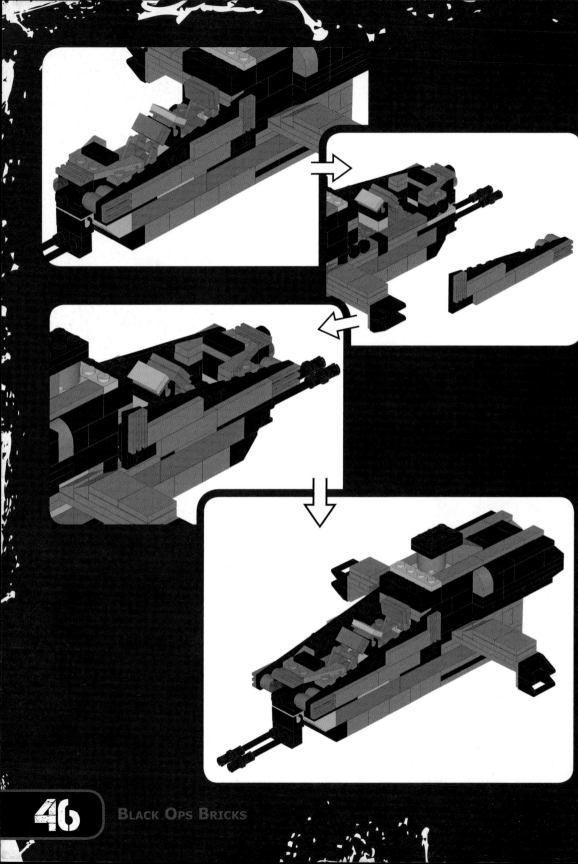

BLACK OPS BRICKS

13

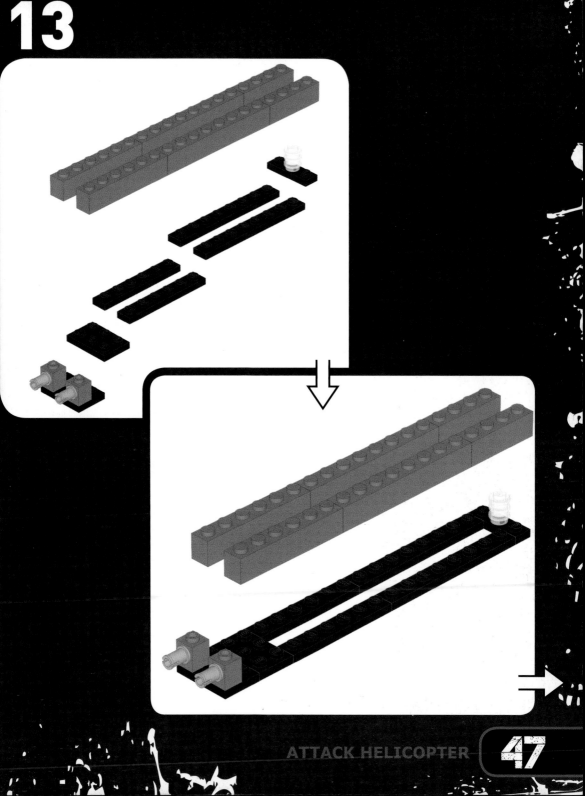

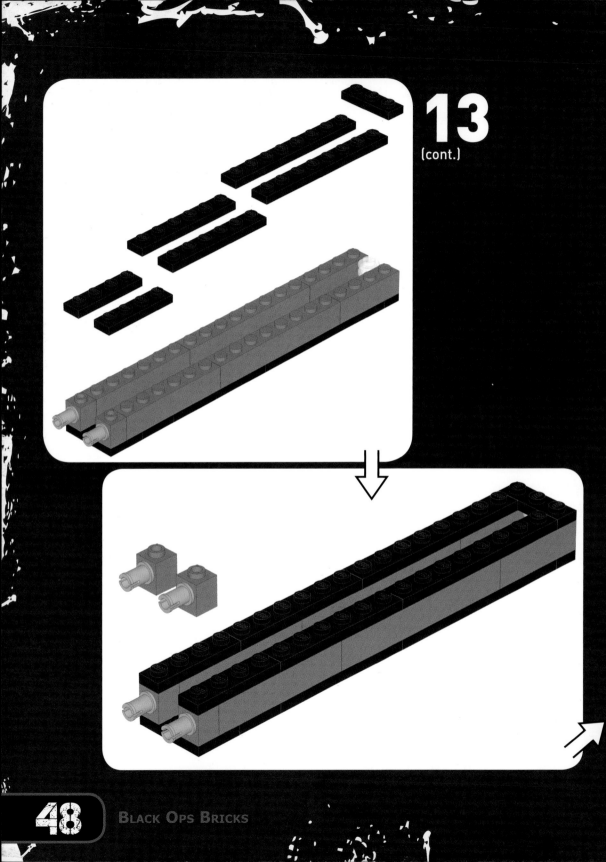

13
(cont.)

BLACK OPS BRICKS

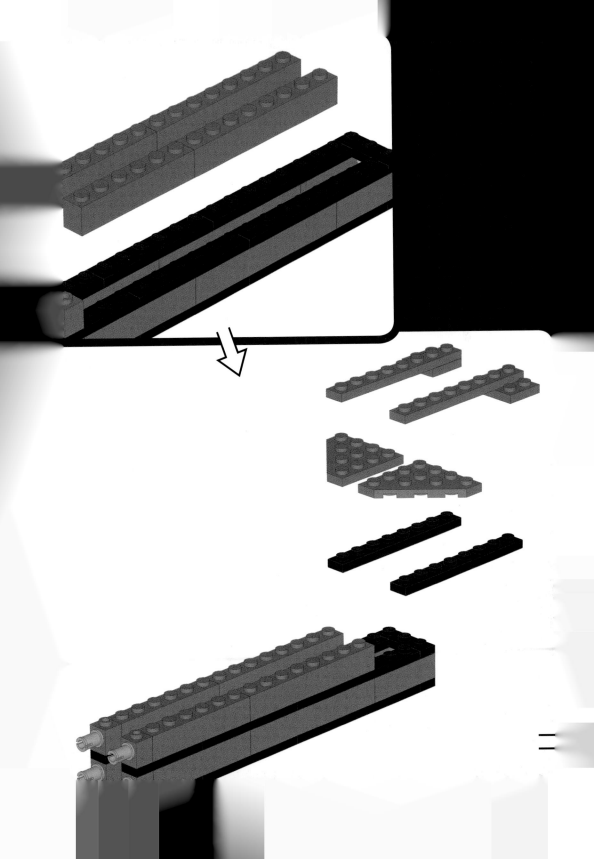

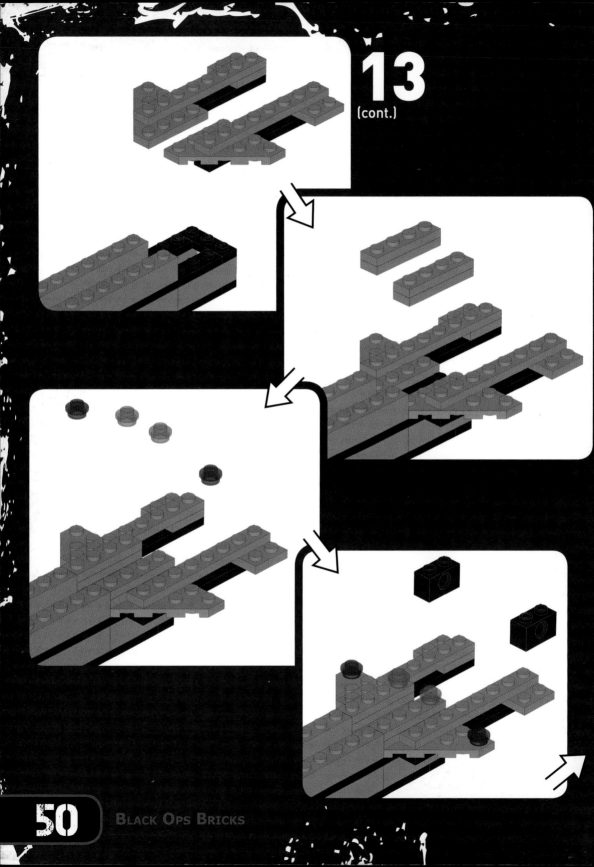

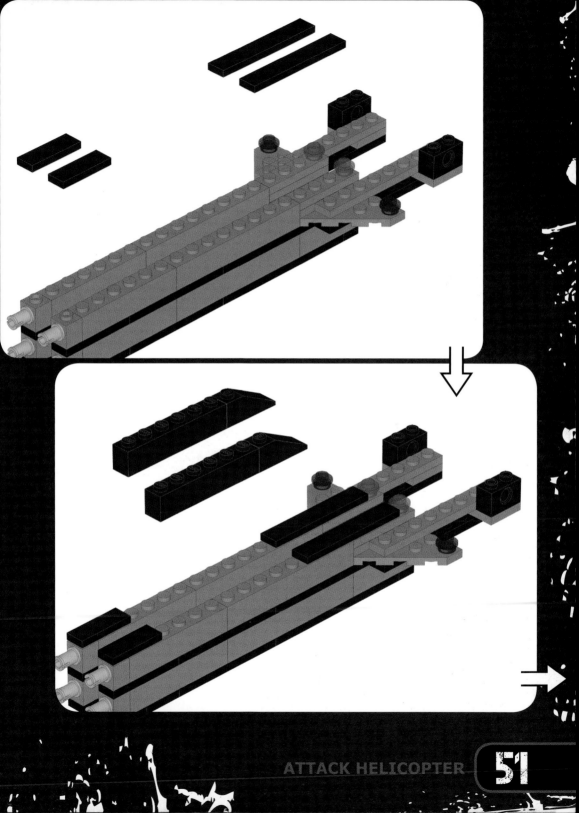

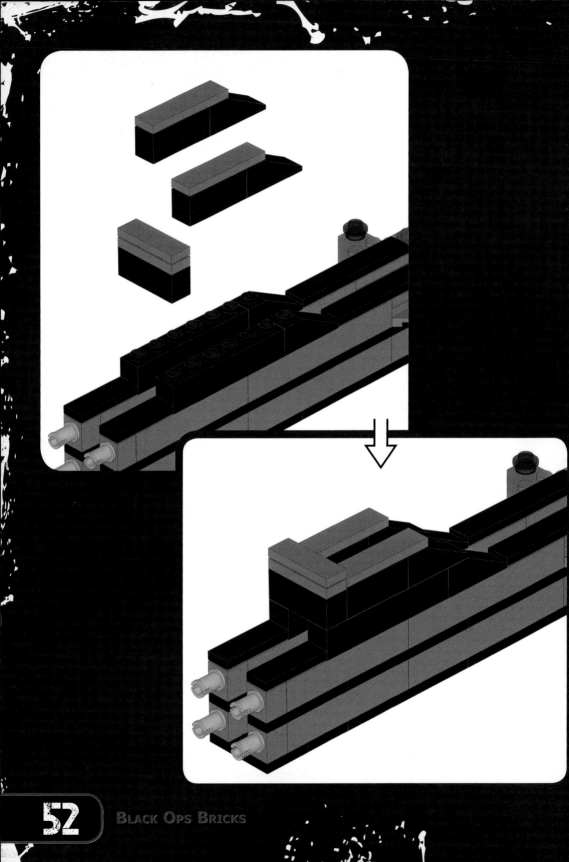

BLACK OPS BRICKS

14

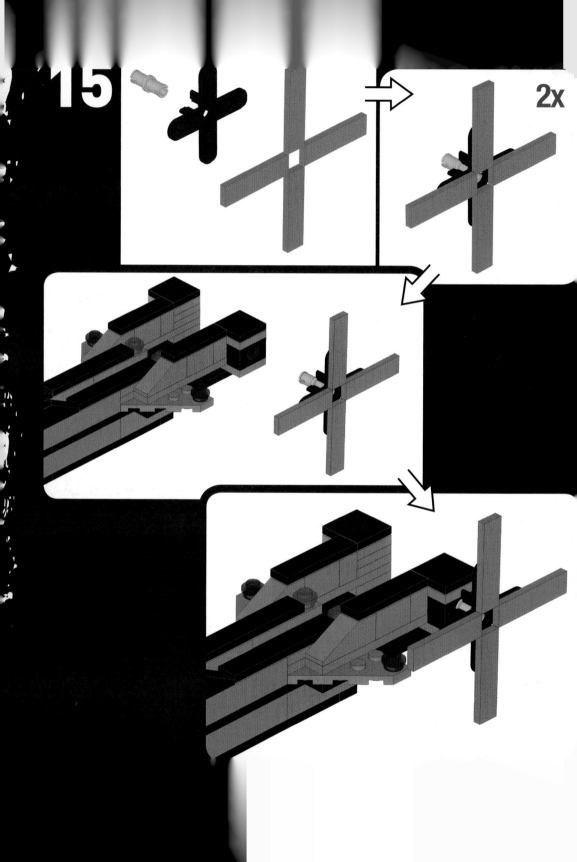

2x

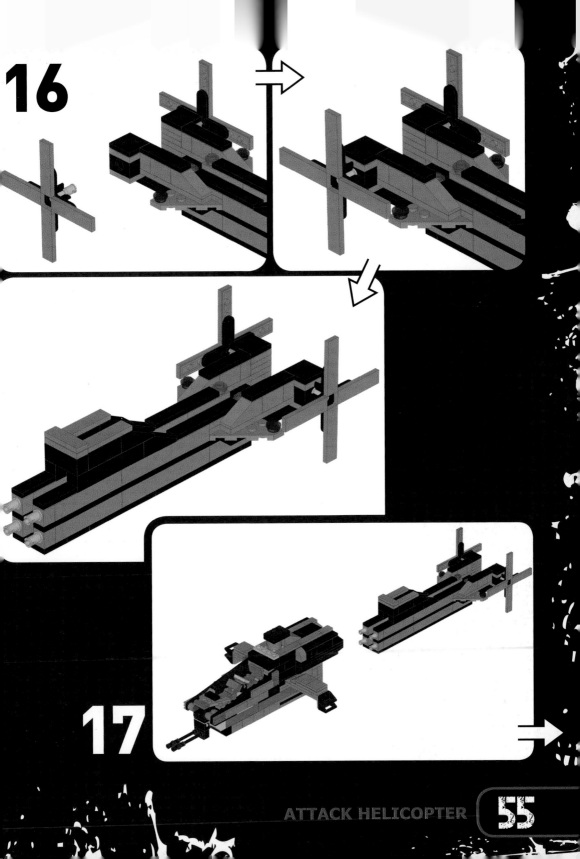

16

17

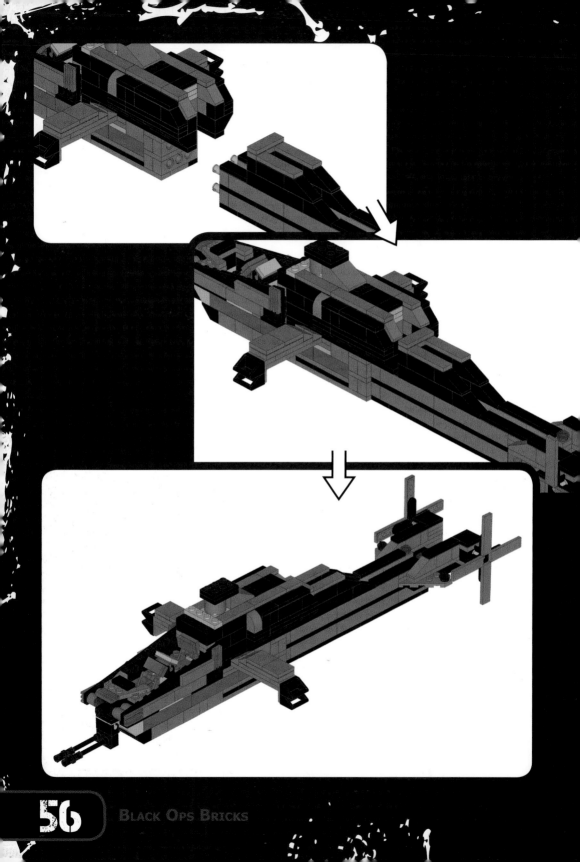

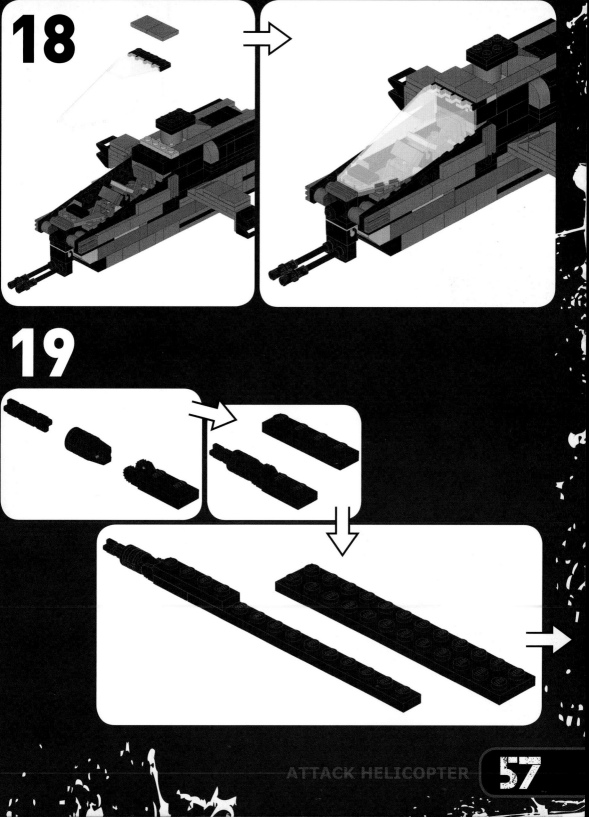

18

19

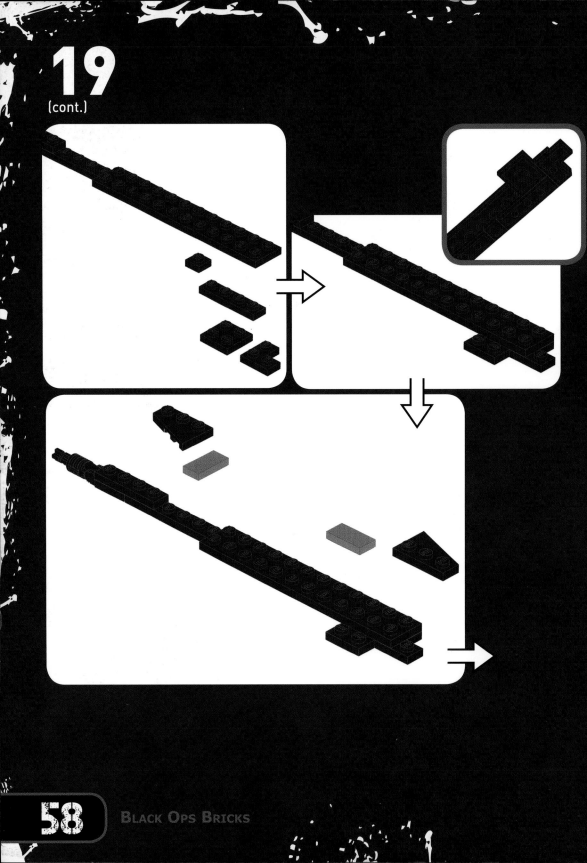

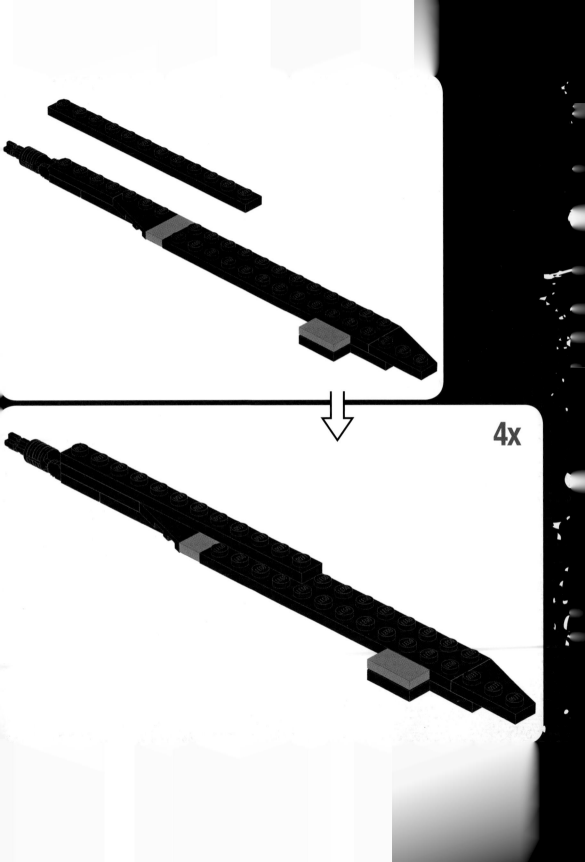

4x

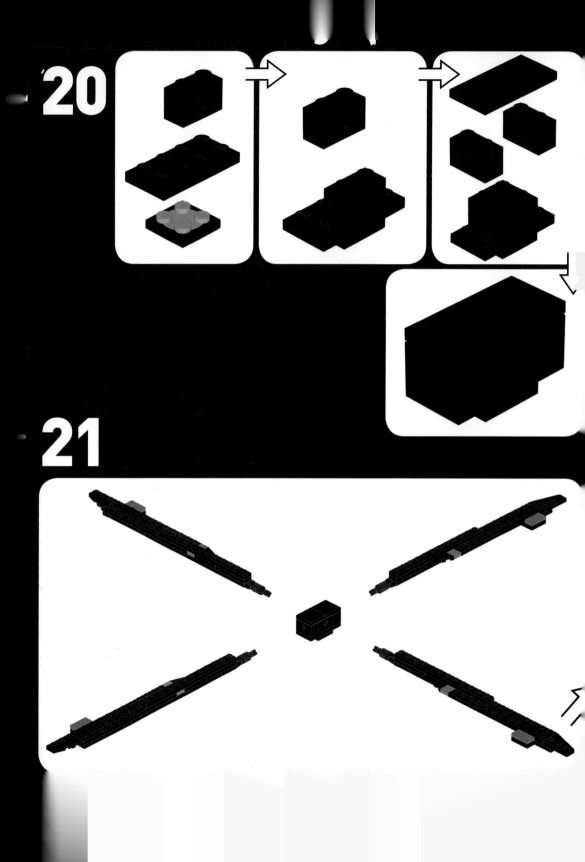

22

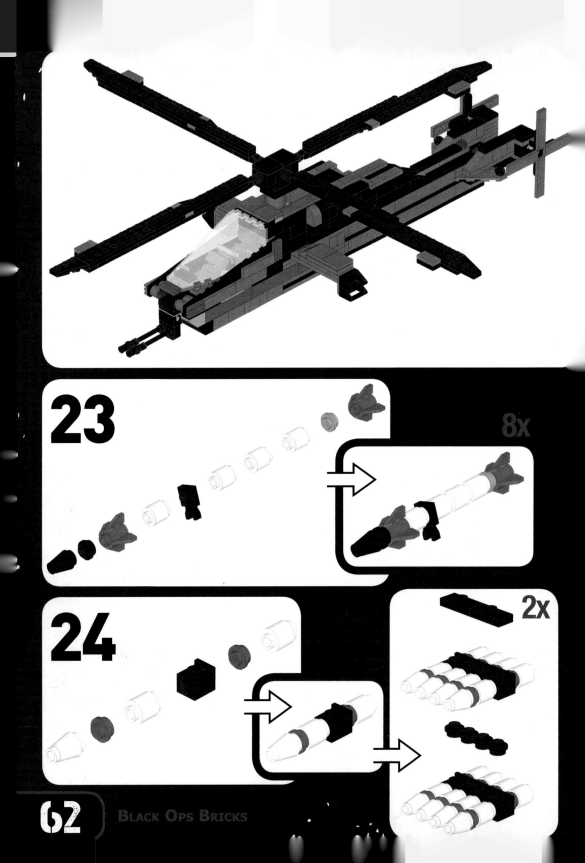

23

8x

24

2x

BLACK OPS BRICKS

25

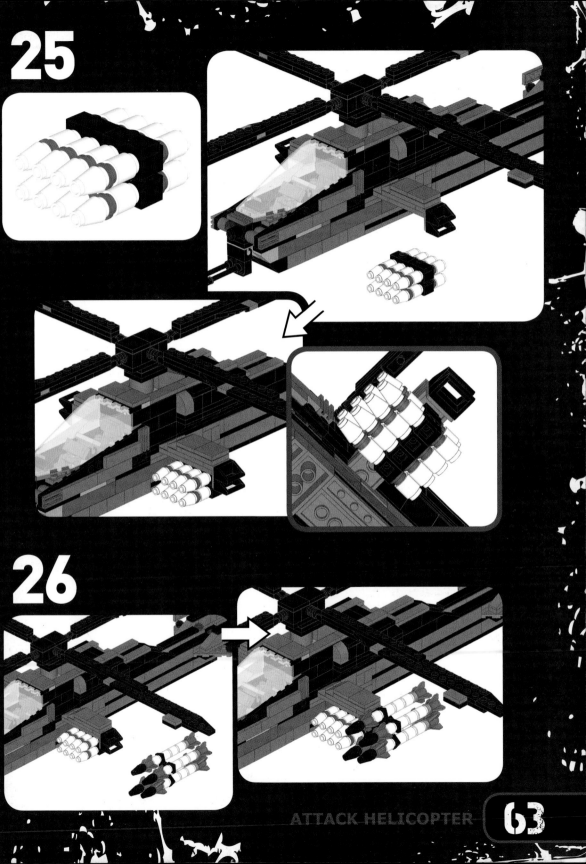

26

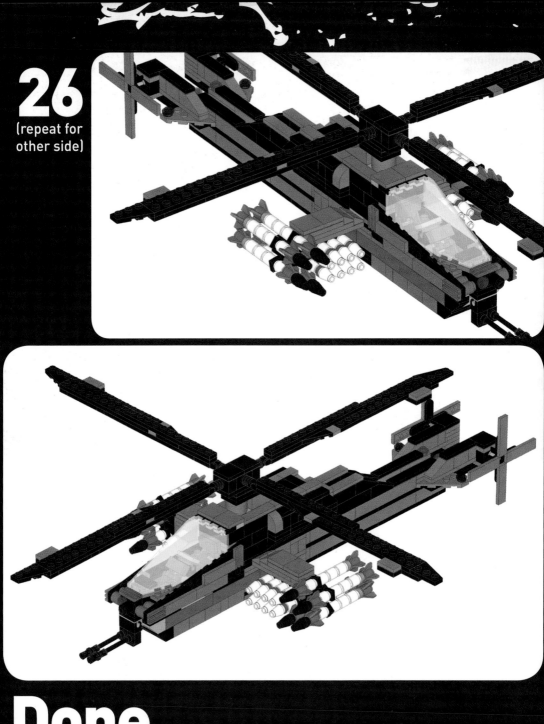

Done

SNUBNOSE OFF-ROADER
(AND LIGHT RE-SUPPLY VEHICLE)

PIECE COUNT:
- 286 elements

FEATURES:
- Trunk for small amounts of supplies
- Reverse-open doors for quick exit

A safe solution for any soldier needing to get anywhere. This vehicle will take you over any terrain and keep you safe inside with reinforced siding and heavy doors.

Being known for durability and being able to take a lot of abuse makes this a popular civilian conversion vehicle.

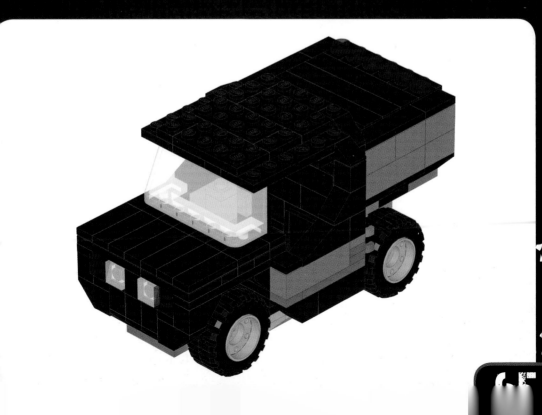

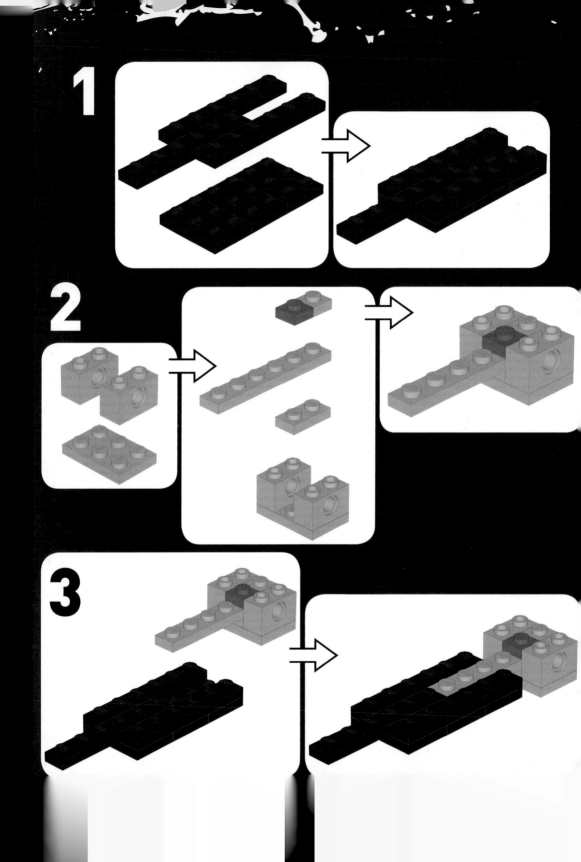

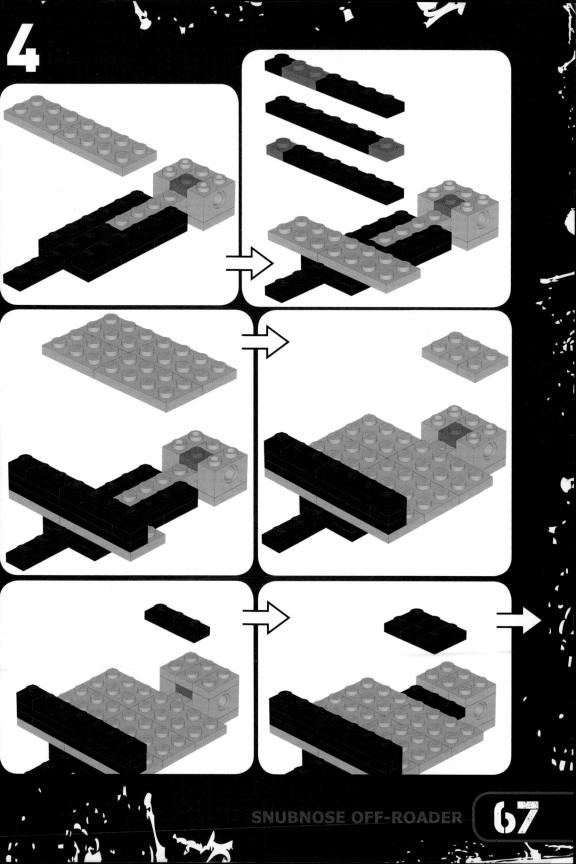

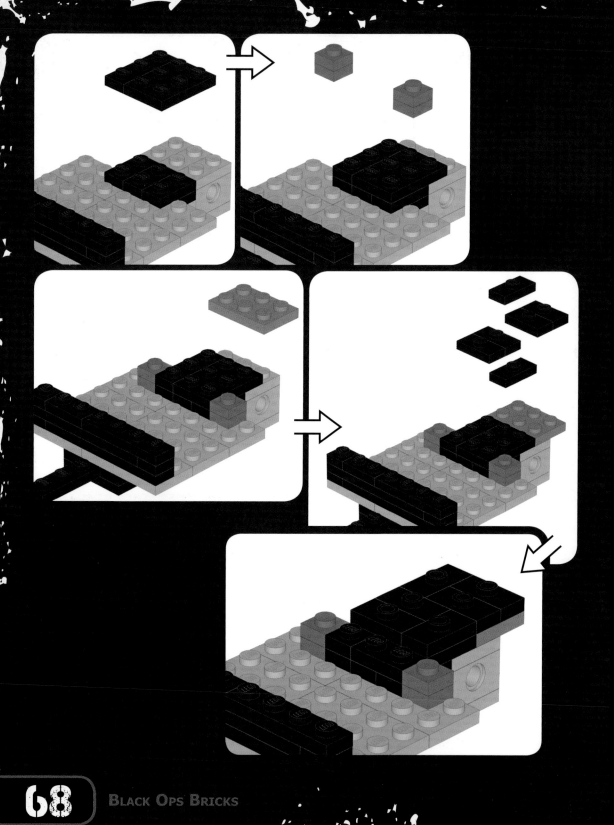

BLACK OPS BRICKS

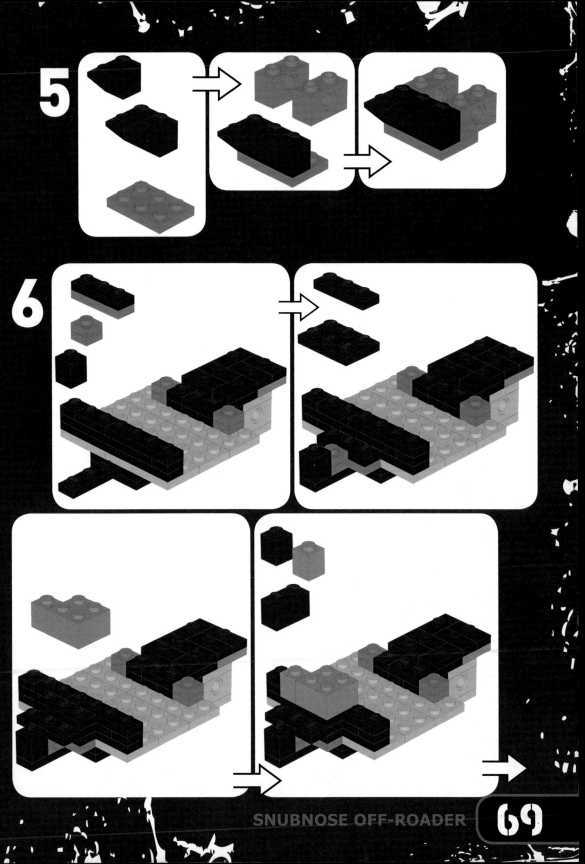

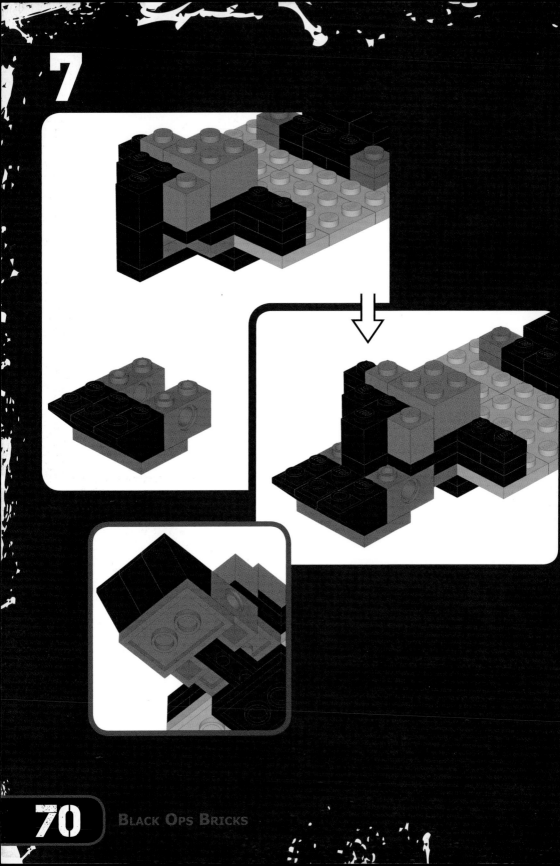

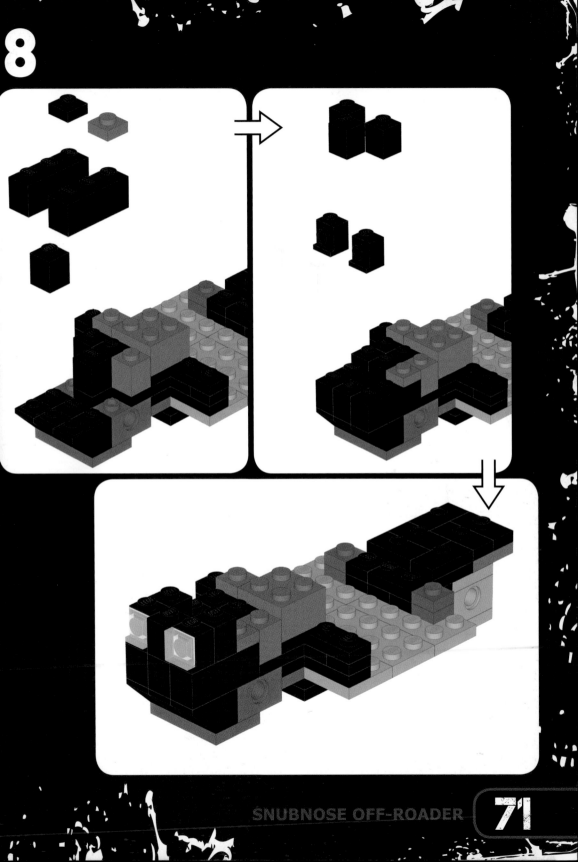

9

10

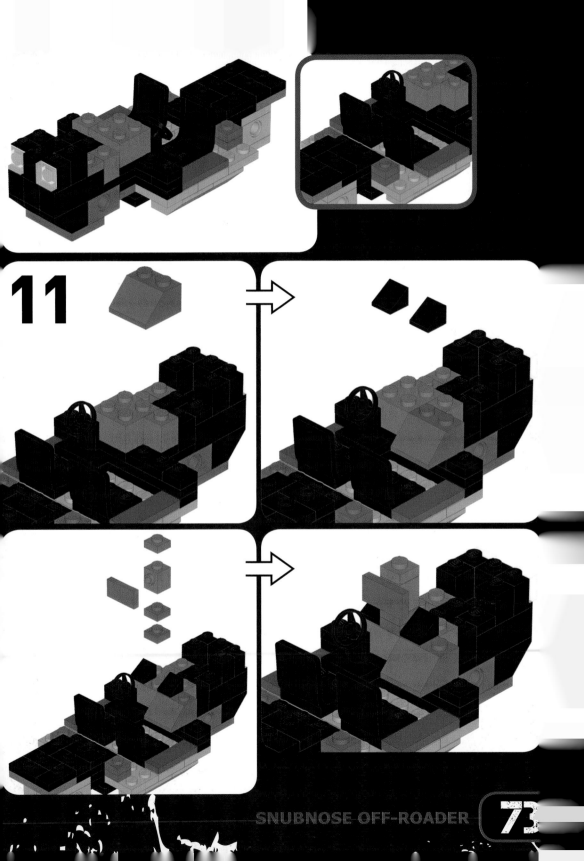

11

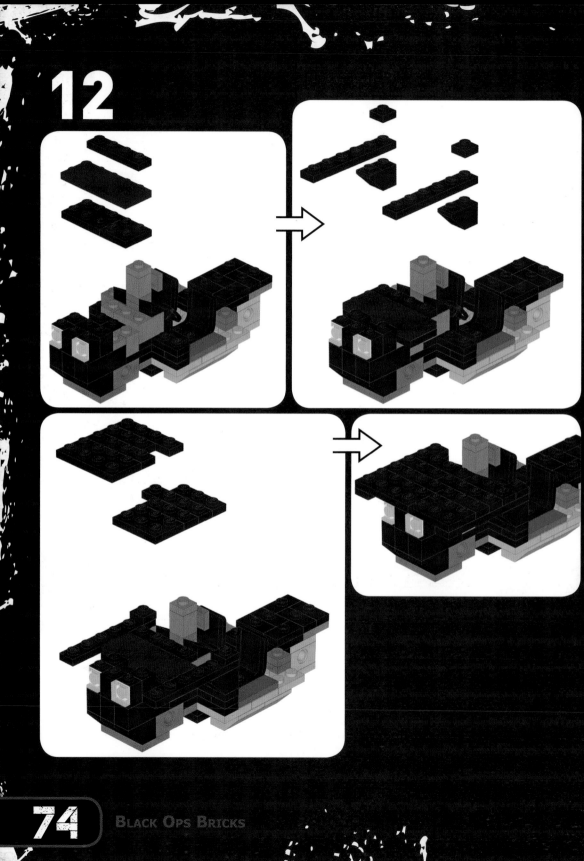

12

BLACK OPS BRICKS

13

14

15

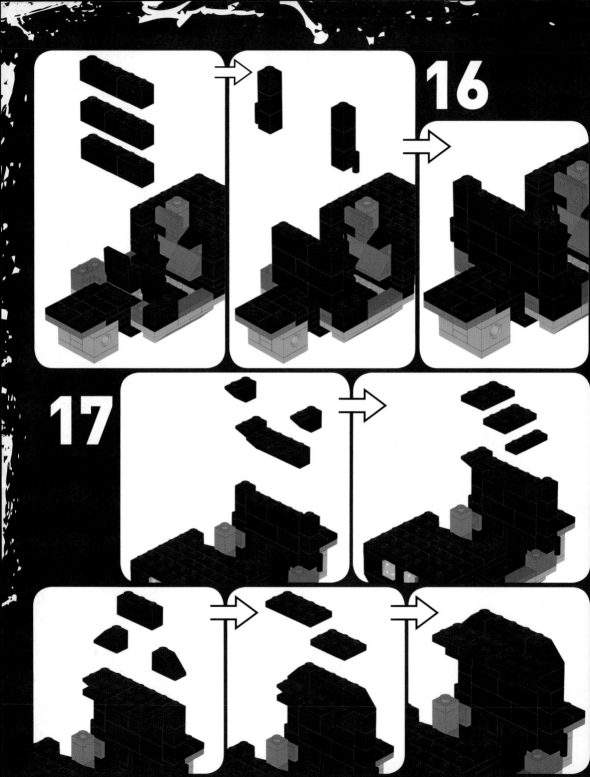

18

19

20

21

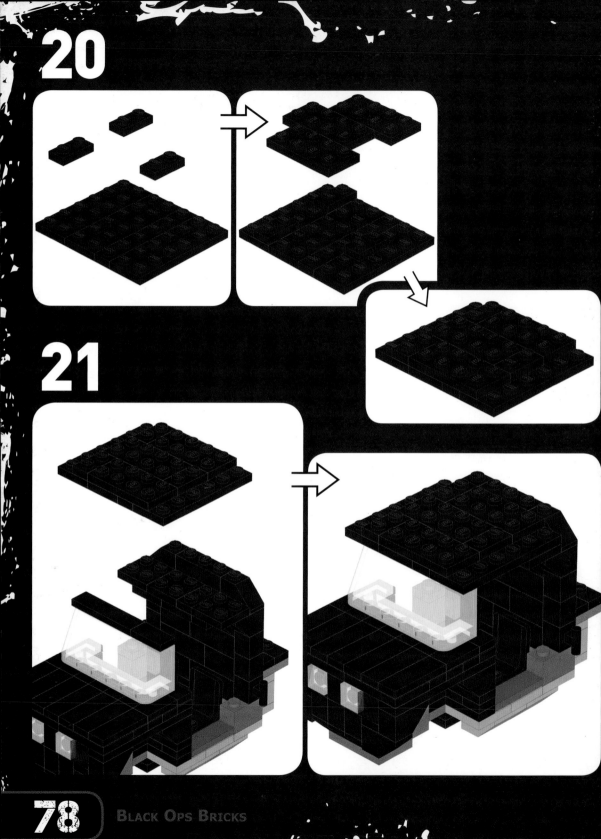

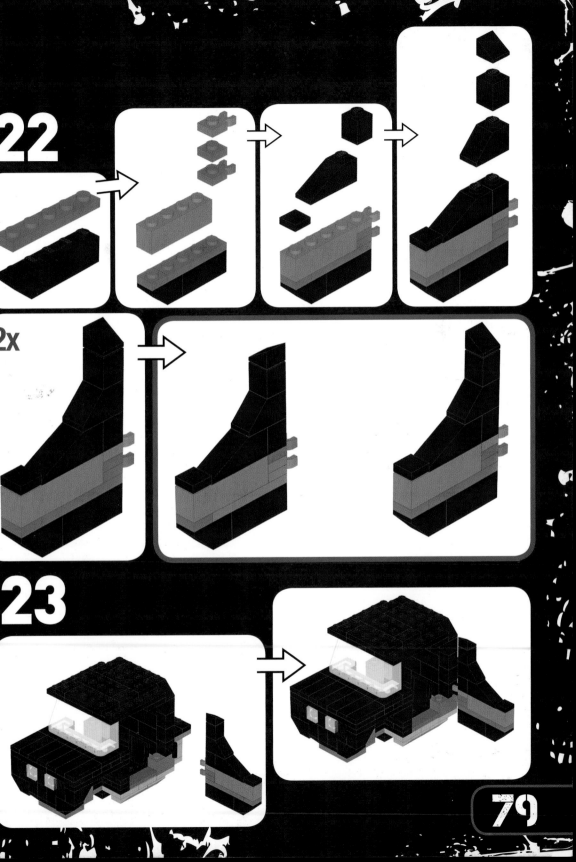

22

2x

23

24

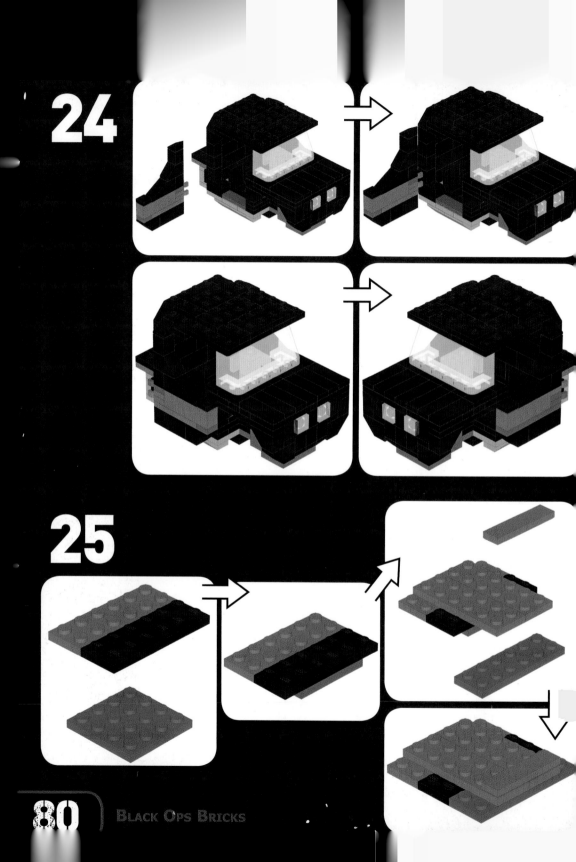

25

BLACK OPS BRICKS

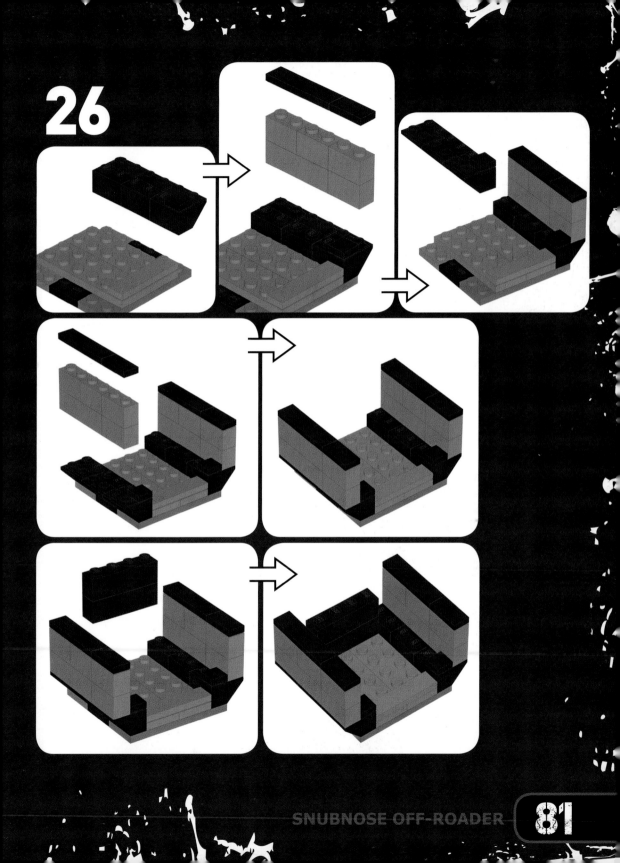

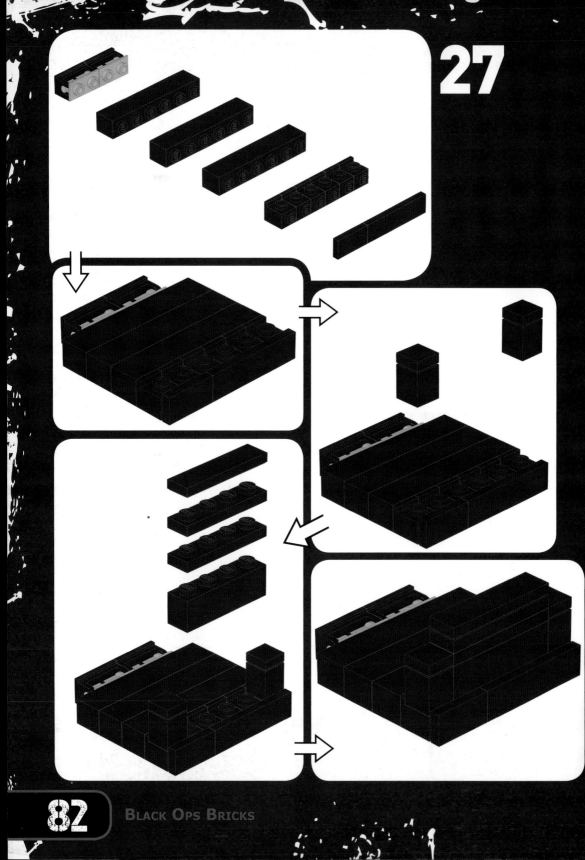

BLACK OPS BRICKS

28

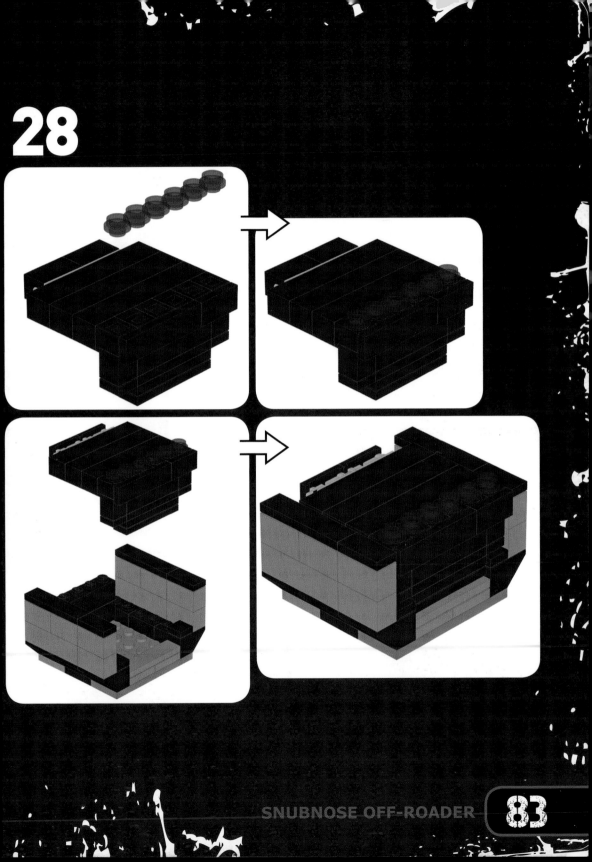

29

Connect the trunk.

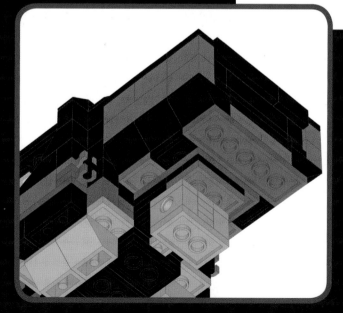

30

4x

31

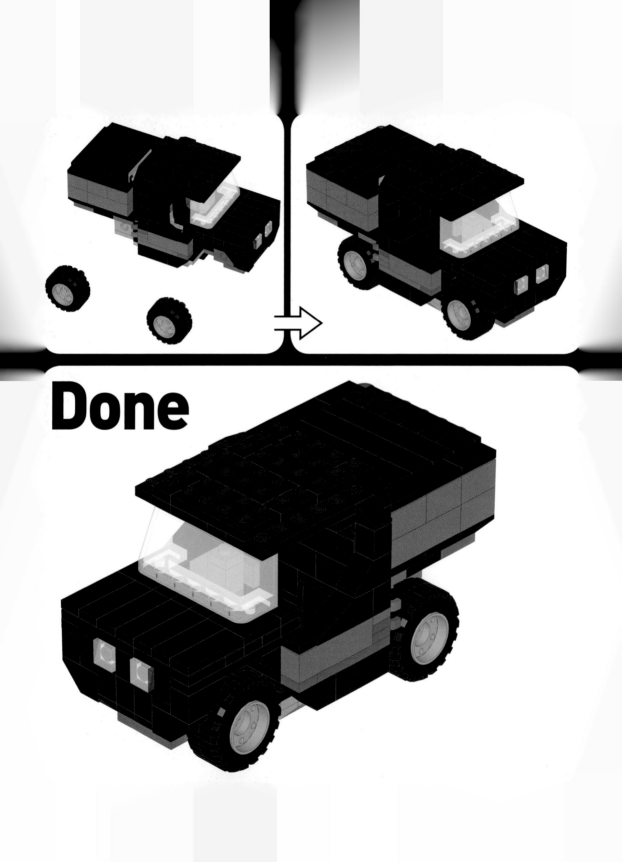

Done

DESERT RECON VEHICLE

PIECE COUNT:
- 166 elements

FEATURES:
- Three person crew
- High ground clearance
- Rear-mounted swiveling cannon
- Souped-up motor

Borrowing its form from popular sand crawlers and dune buggies, this extra fast recon vehicle will send you soaring off sand dunes.

Popular with elite special forces due to its powerful yet quiet motor, it will get you in and out of a bad situation before the enemy even realizes you were there.

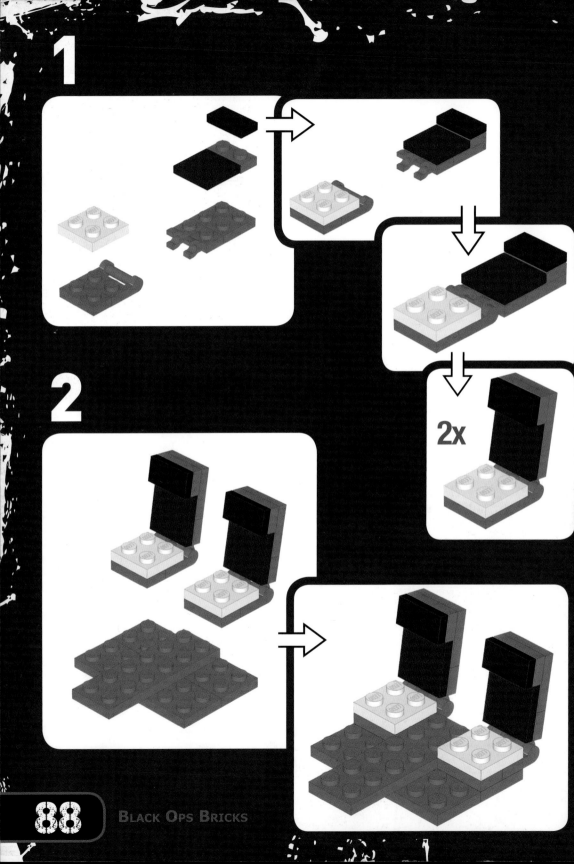

1

2

2x

3

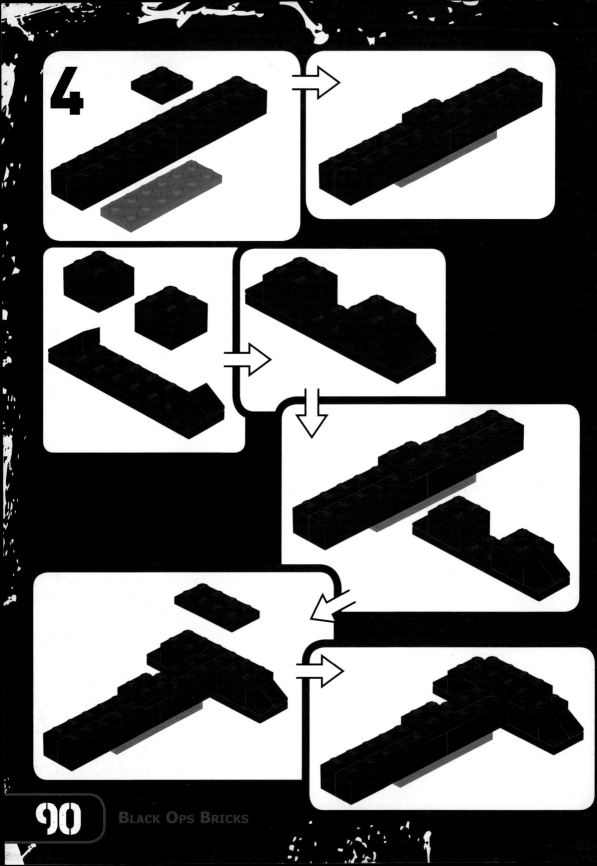

4

BLACK OPS BRICKS

5

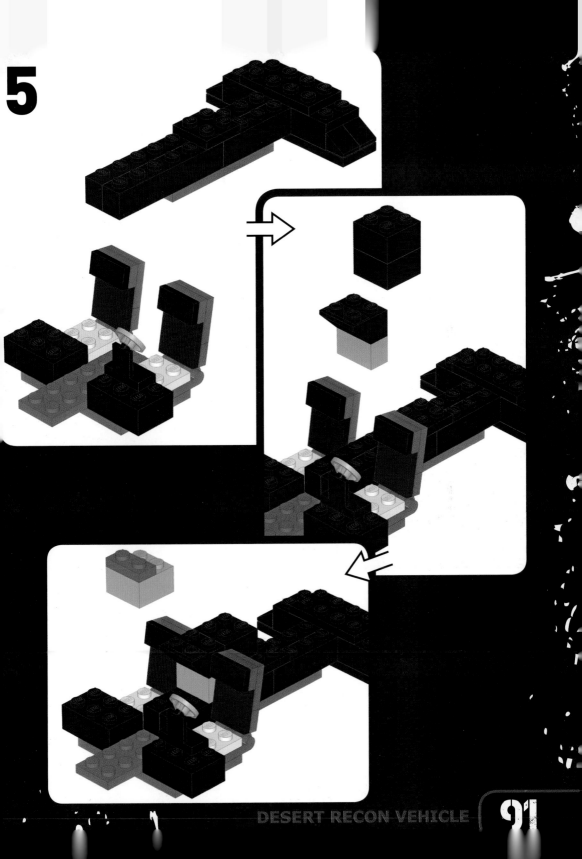

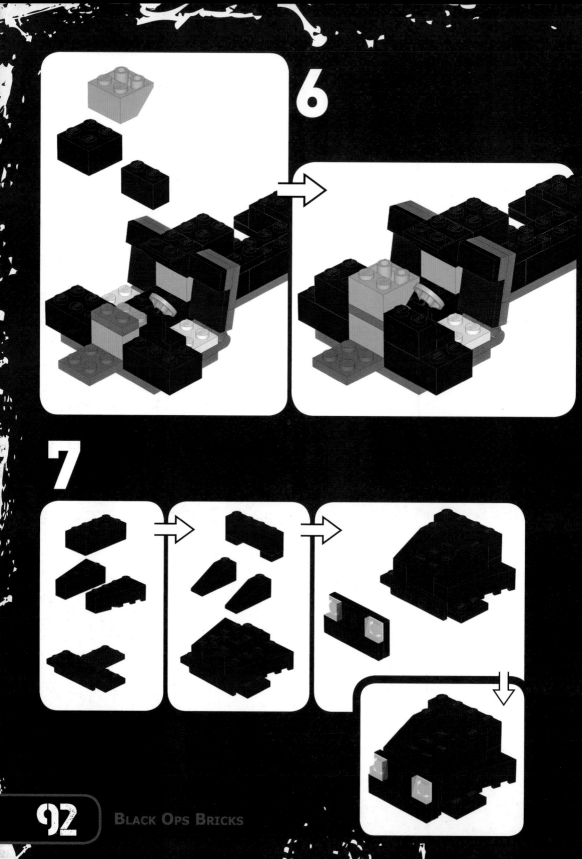

8

9

10

11

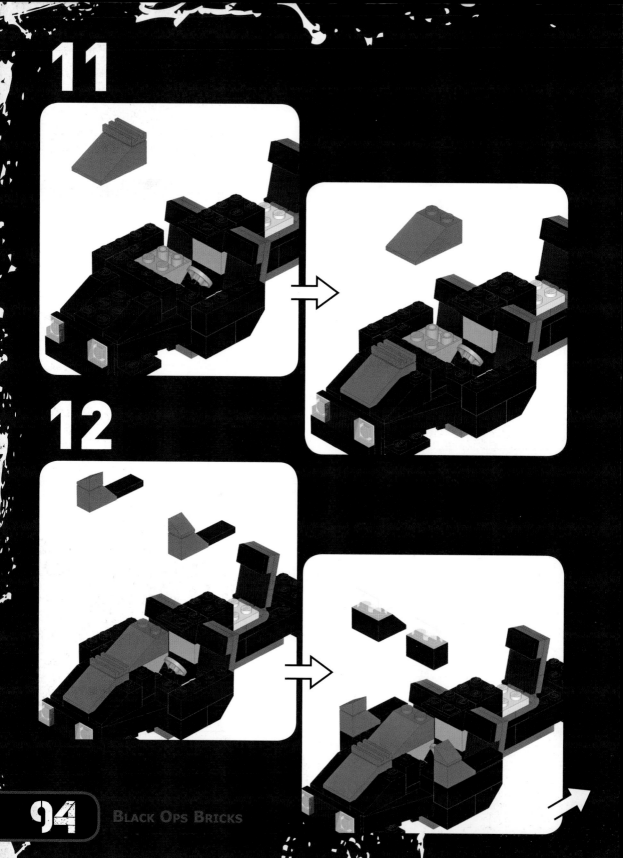

12

BLACK OPS BRICKS

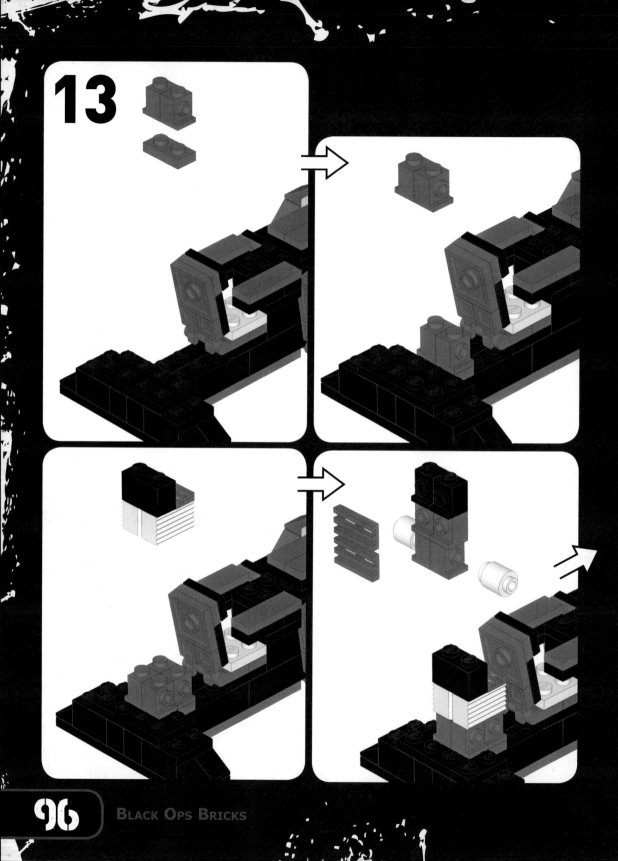

13

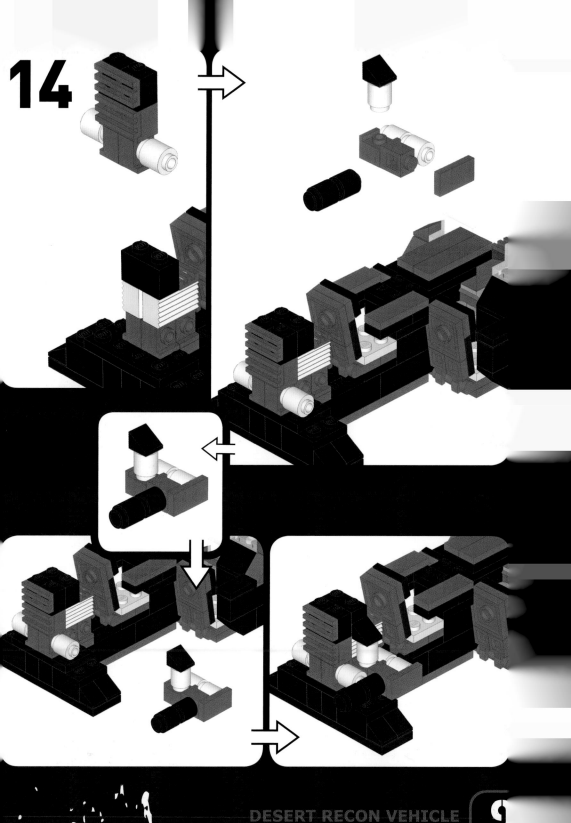

14

15

16

17

4x

Done

ARMORED TRANSPORT

Piece Count:
- 535 elements

Features:
- Front plow
- Back lift gate
- Door weapon ports
- Reinforced armor
- National pride

This armored truck is for sensitive transport missions where the cargo must be absolutely secure. This beast can have its tires blown off but that doesn't mean the enemy is any more likely to get inside.

Used for cargo transport and as a troop transport for SWAT-type missions.

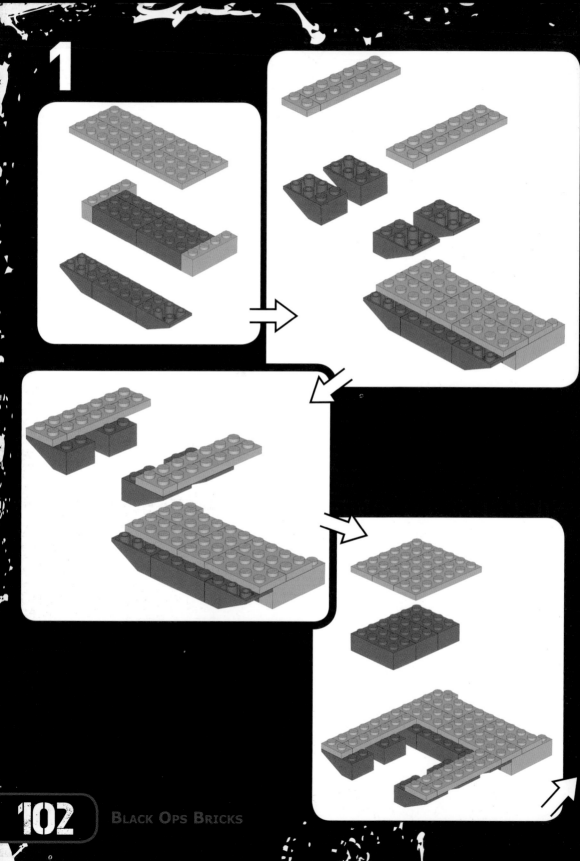

1

BLACK OPS BRICKS

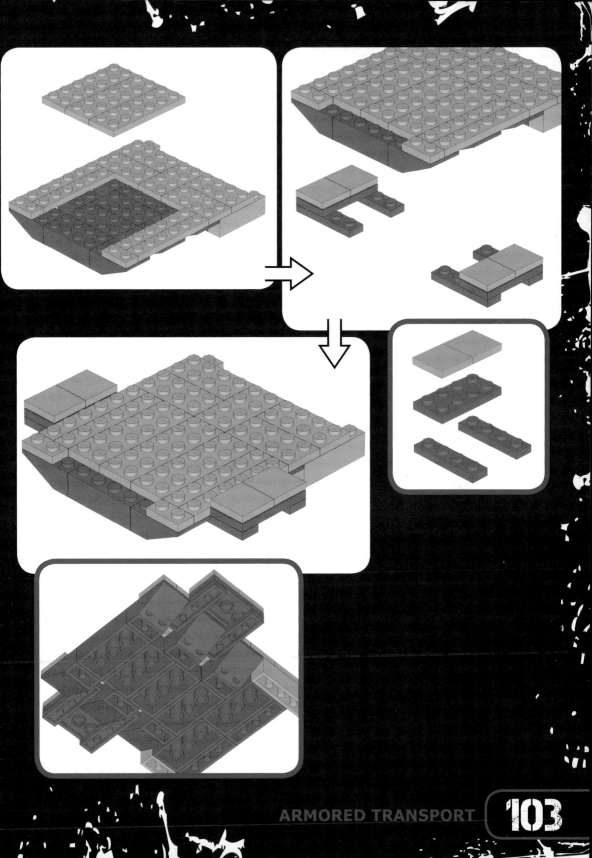

2

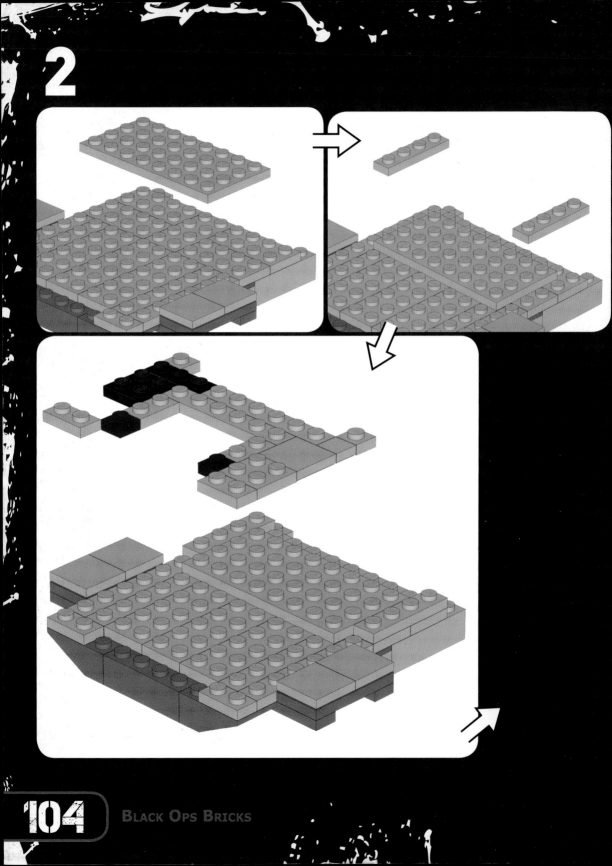

3

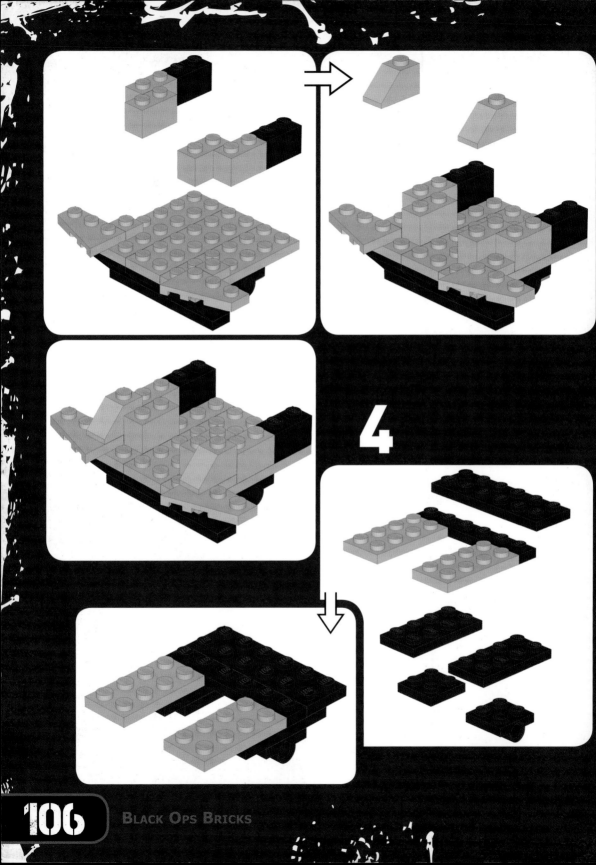

4

BLACK OPS BRICKS

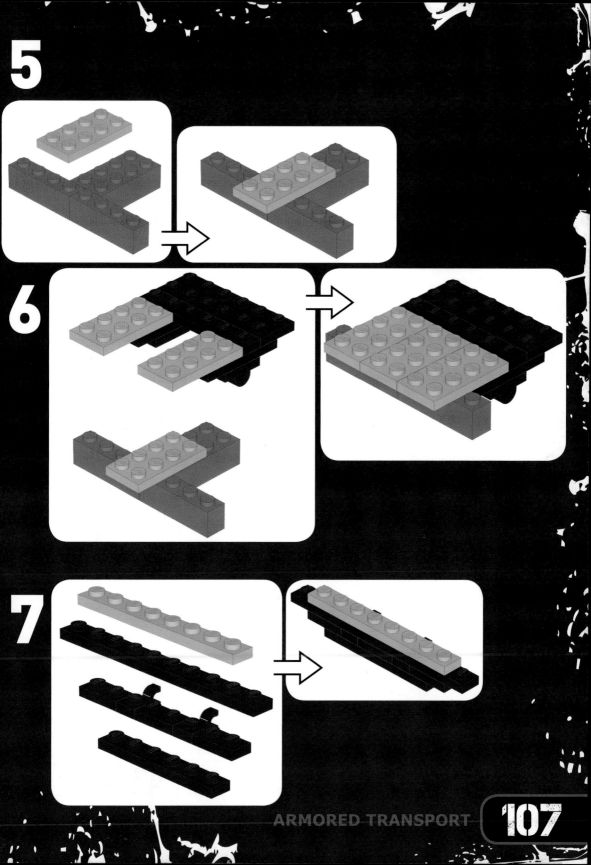

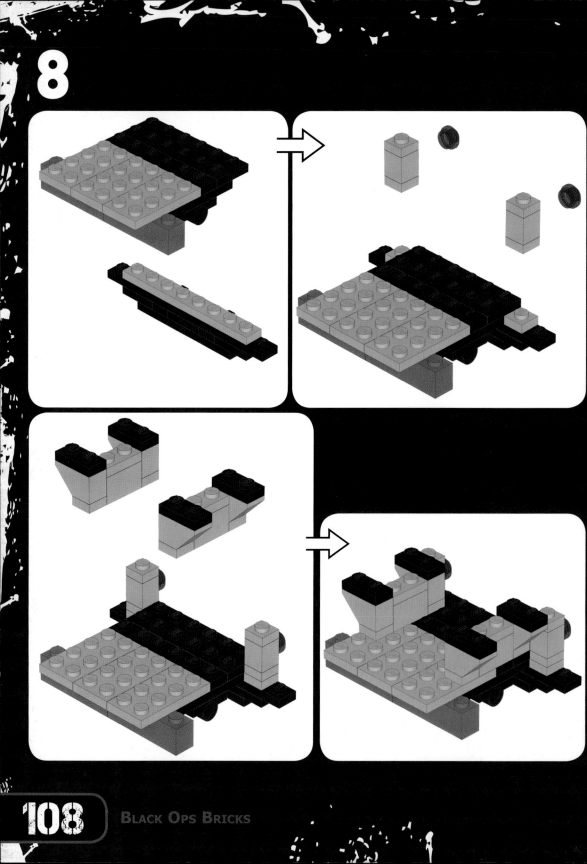

BLACK OPS BRICKS

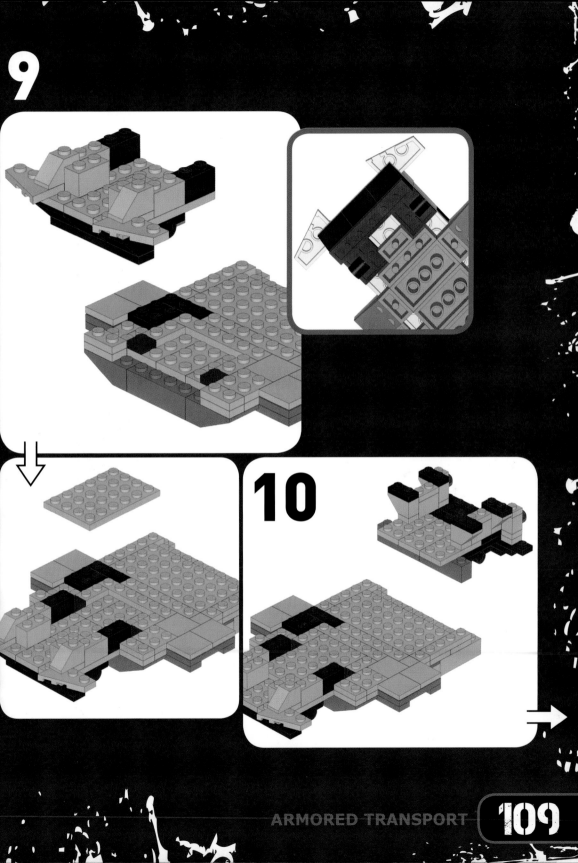

BLACK OPS BRICKS

12

BLACK OPS BRICKS

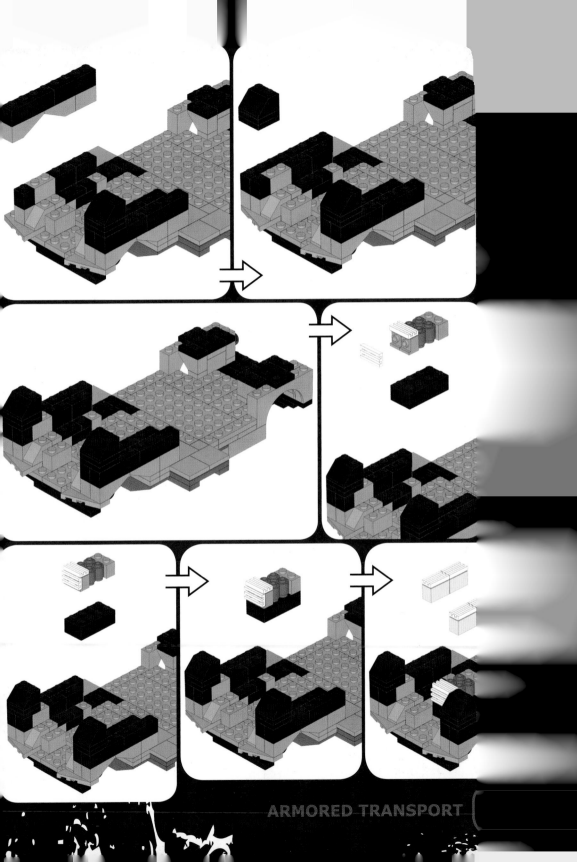

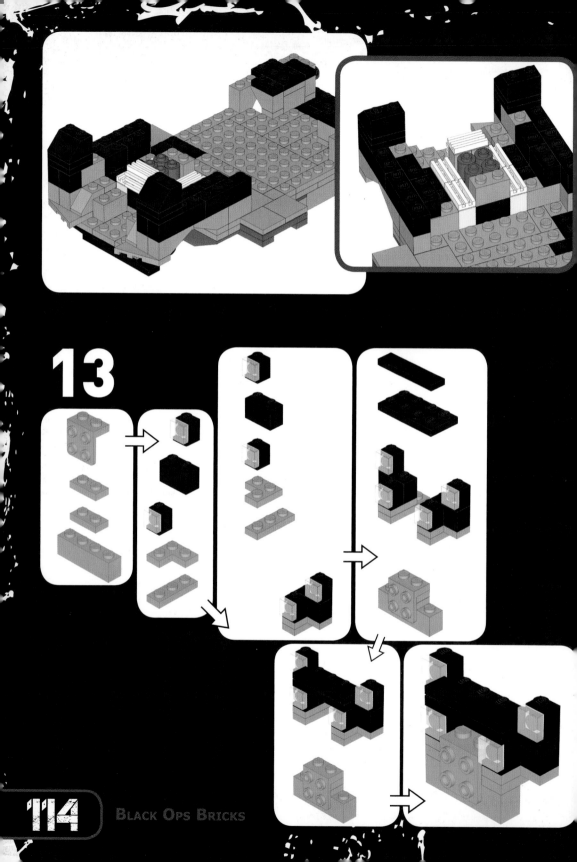

13

BLACK OPS BRICKS

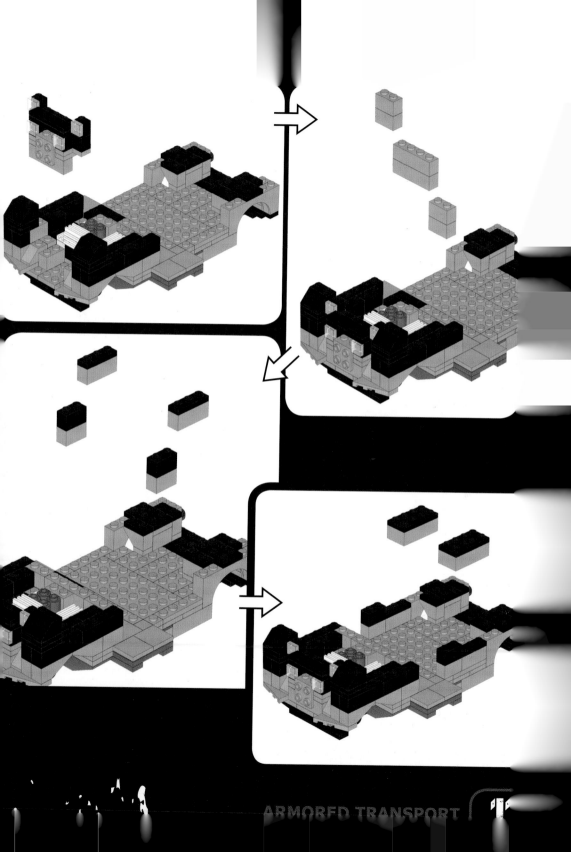

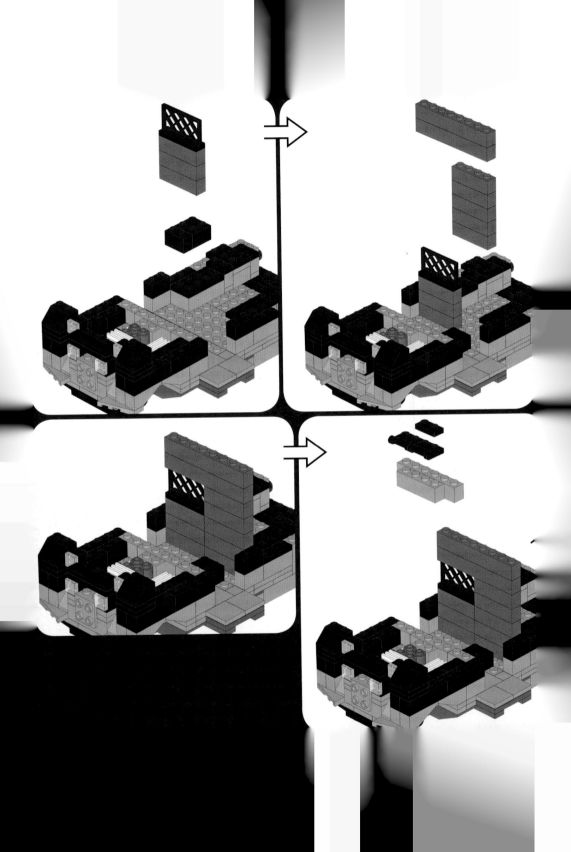

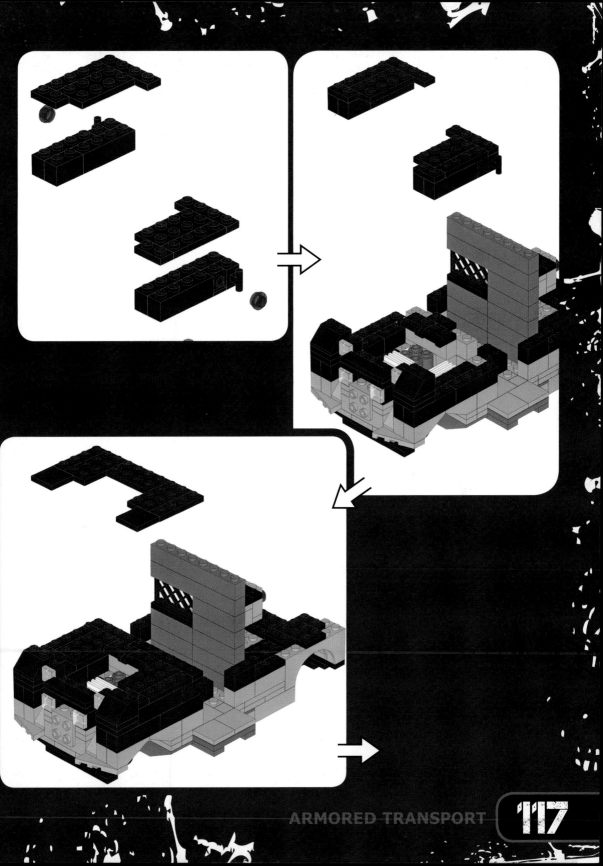

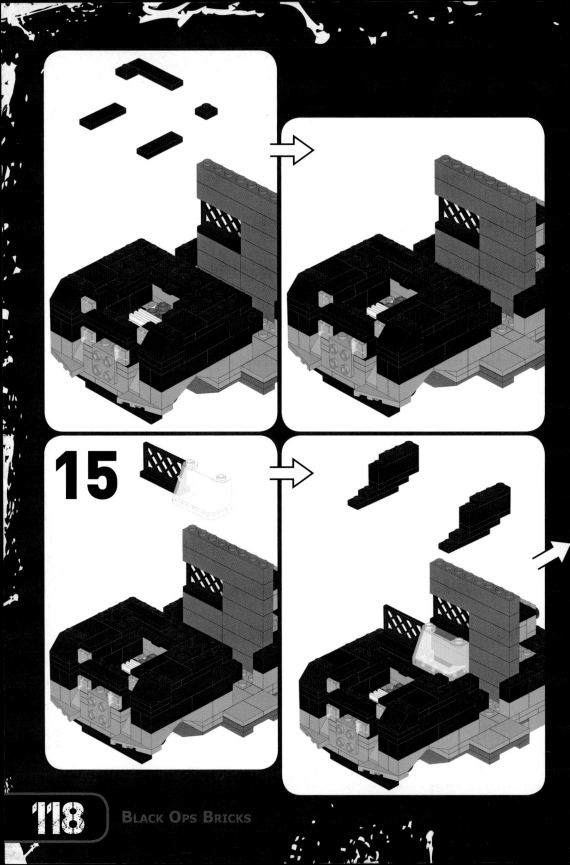

15

BLACK OPS BRICKS

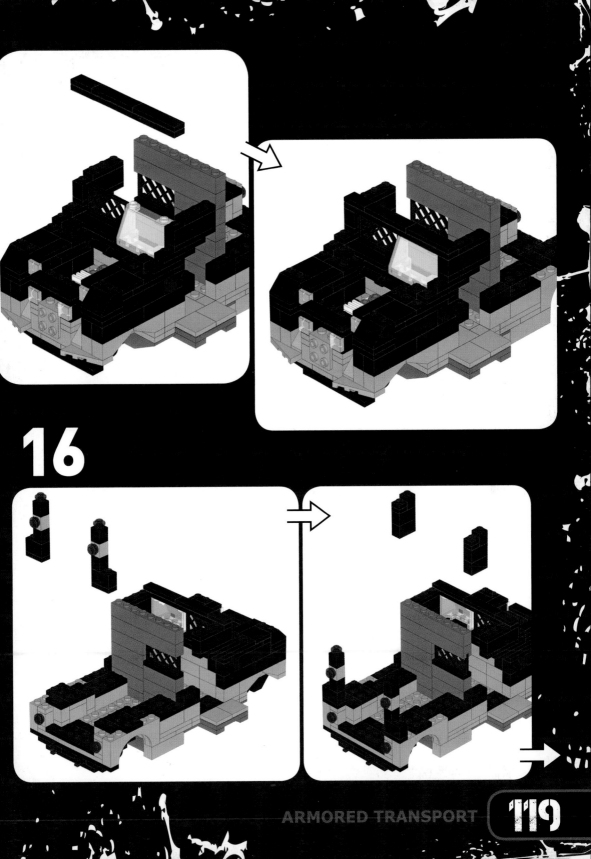

16

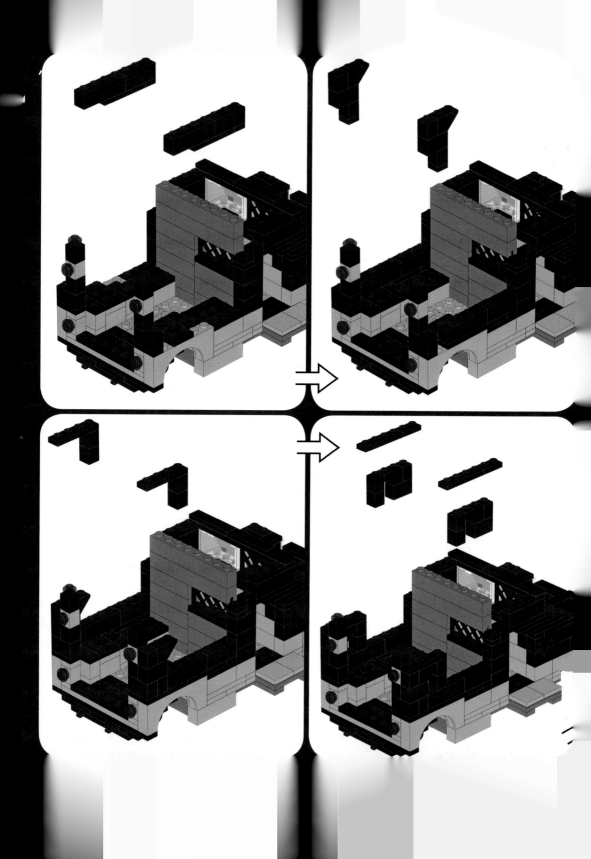

17

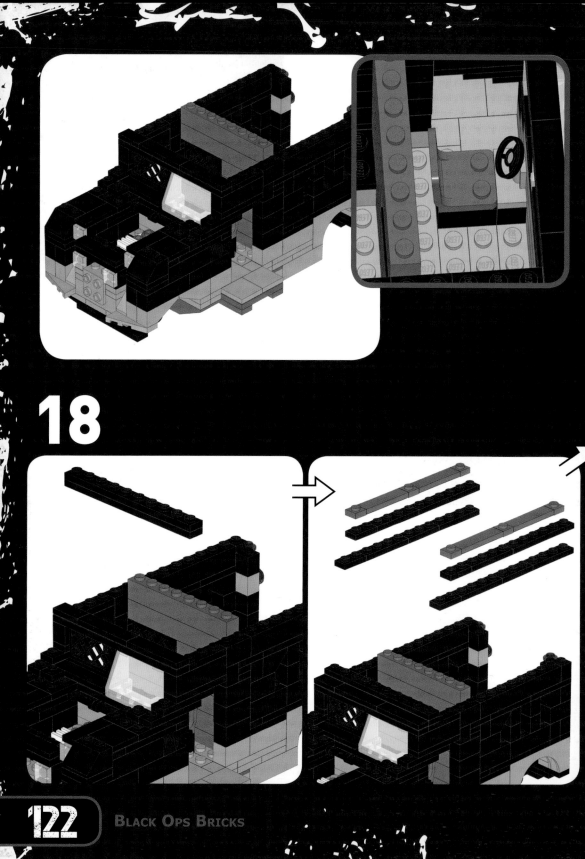

18

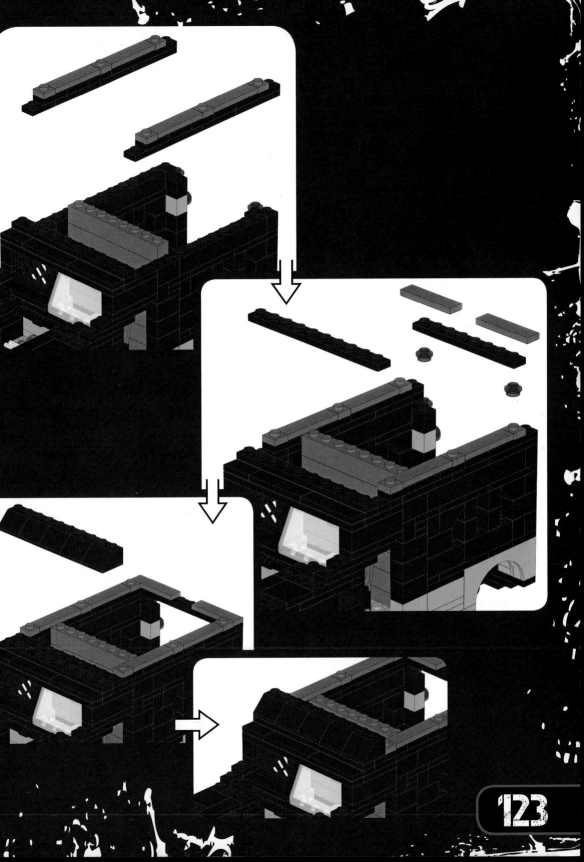

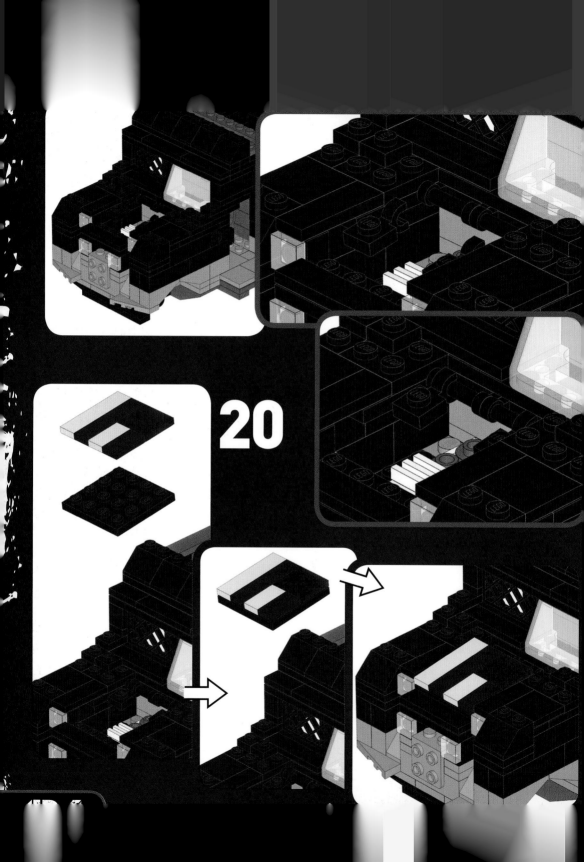

20

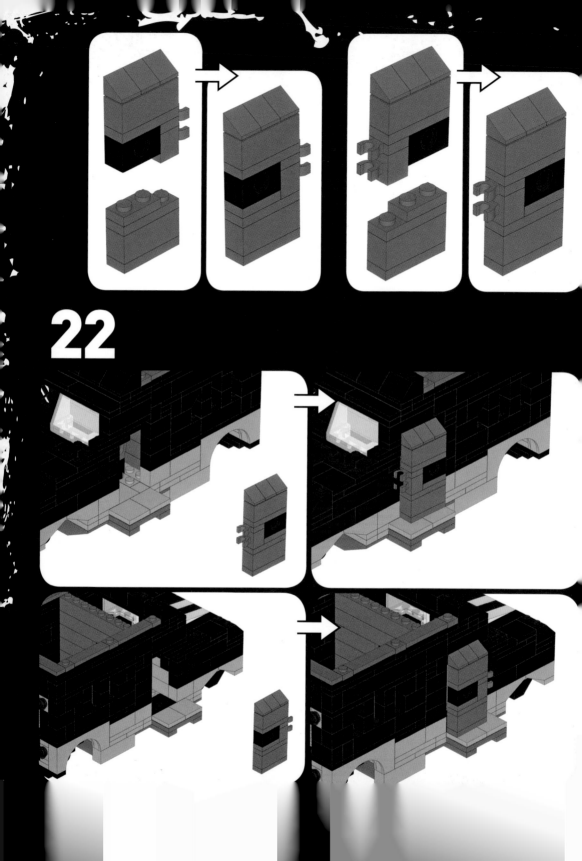

22

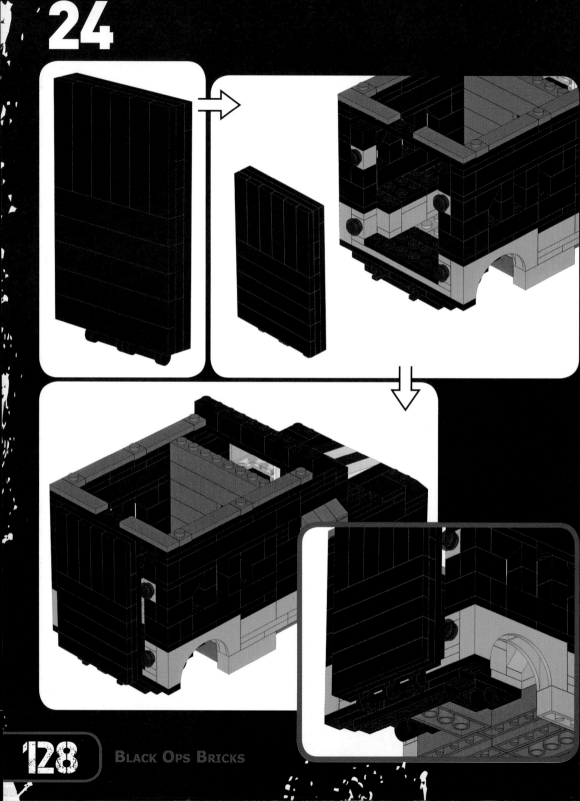

BLACK OPS BRICKS

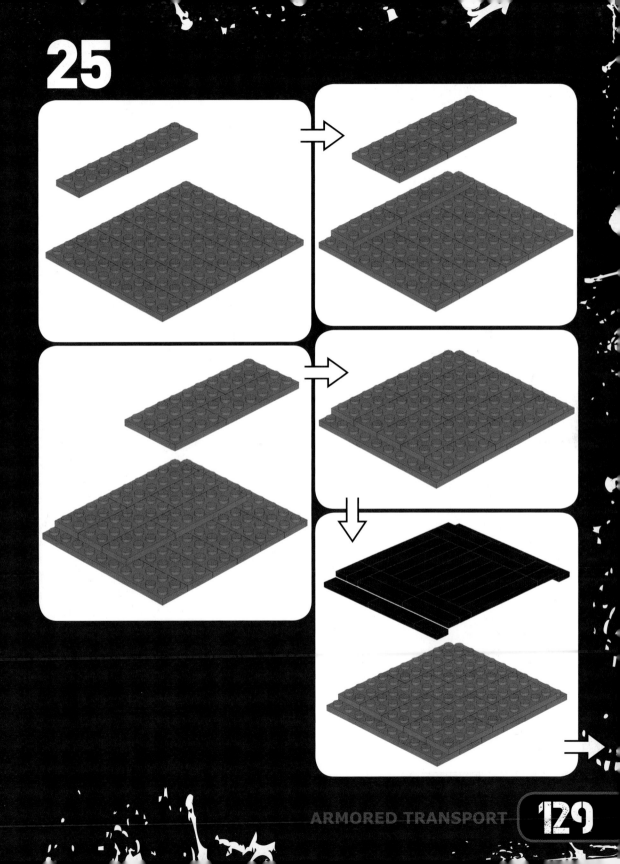

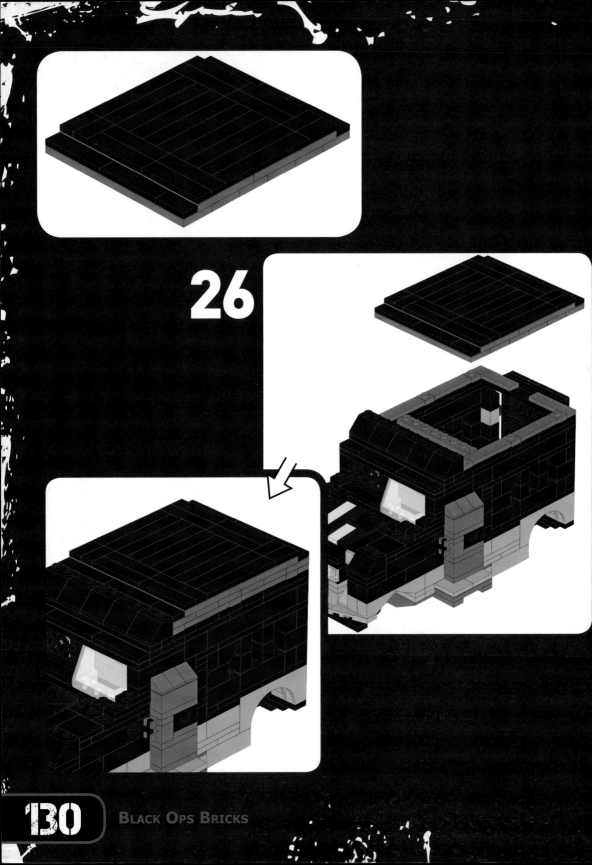

26

BLACK OPS BRICKS

27

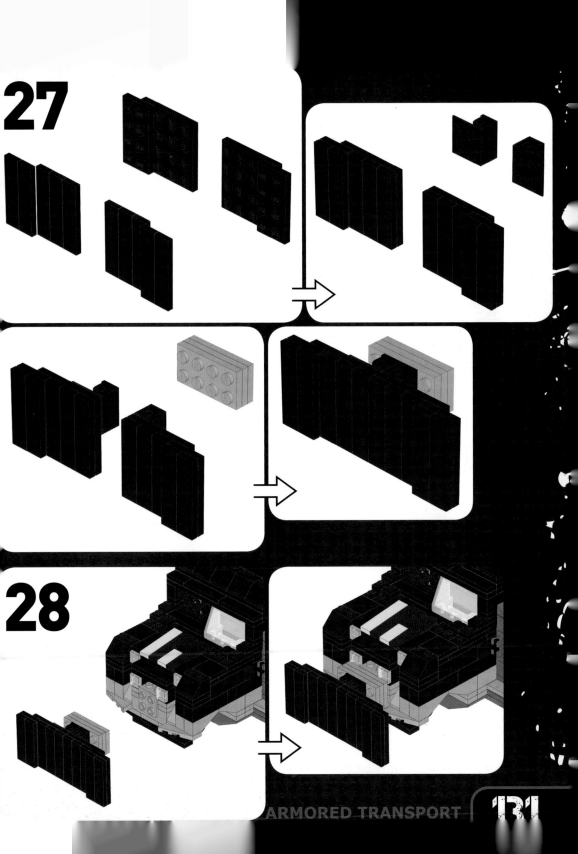

28

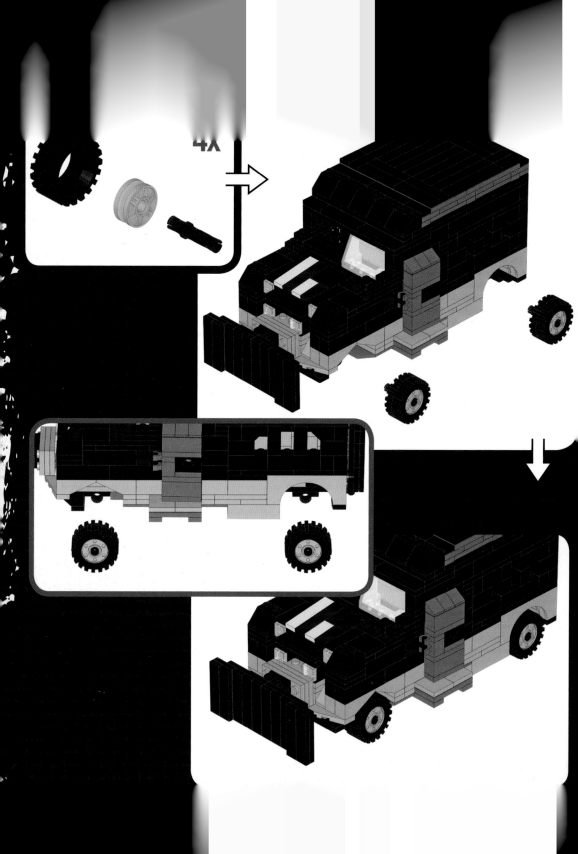

4x

Done

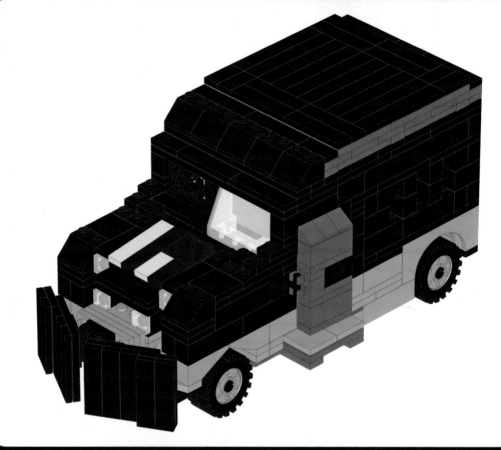

BACKUP HELICOPTER

PIECE COUNT:
593 elements

FEATURES:
Opening side bay door
Swiveling gunner position
Wing-mounted guns
Multiple seats to bring a
backup crew

What will be coming over the horizon to cover you at the LZ from an oncoming horde while you load up the last of the comm gear? This chopper.

With multiple seats, reinforced construction, and enough guns to really get the party started, this thing put the Blackhawk in retirement.

BLACK OPS BRICKS

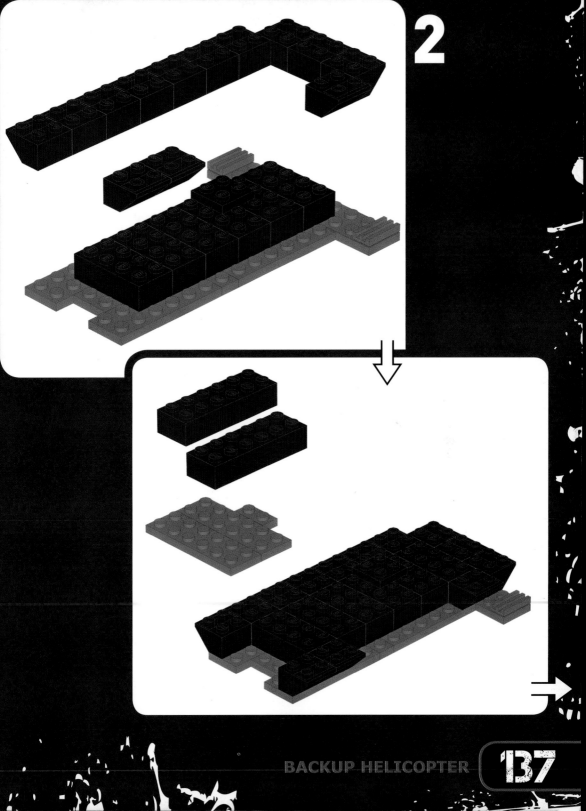

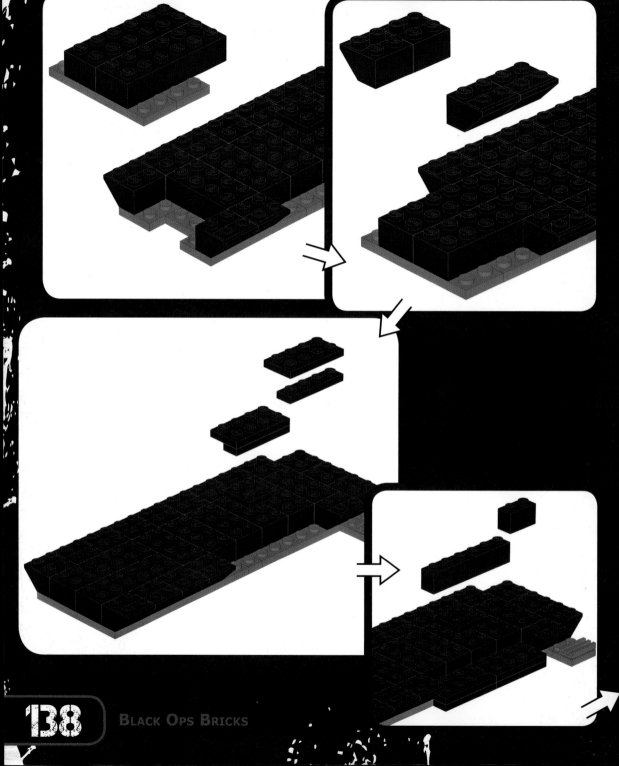

BLACK OPS BRICKS

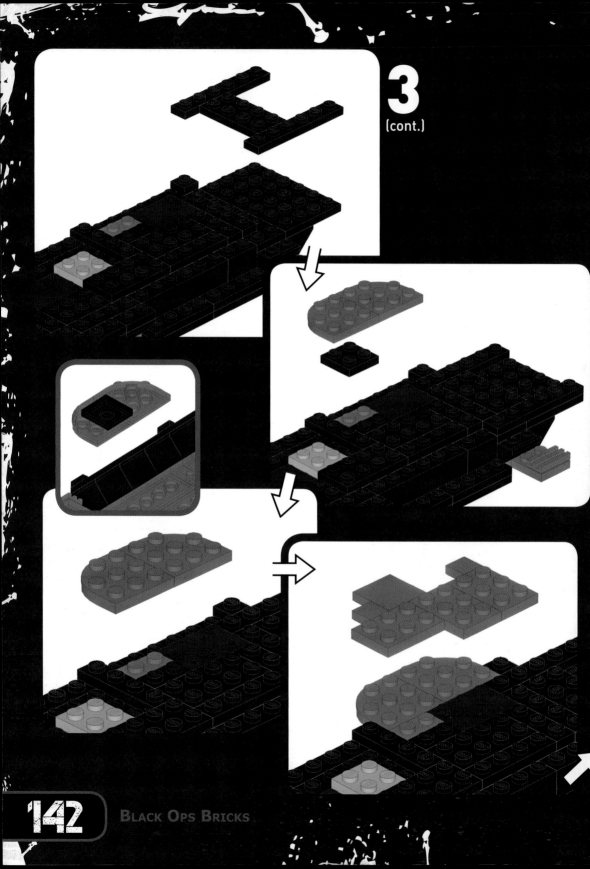

3
(cont.)

BLACK OPS BRICKS

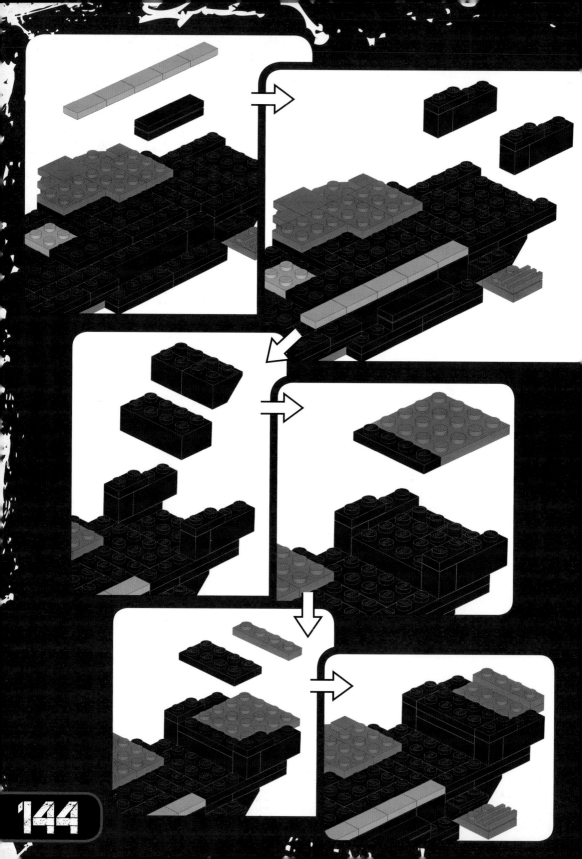

5

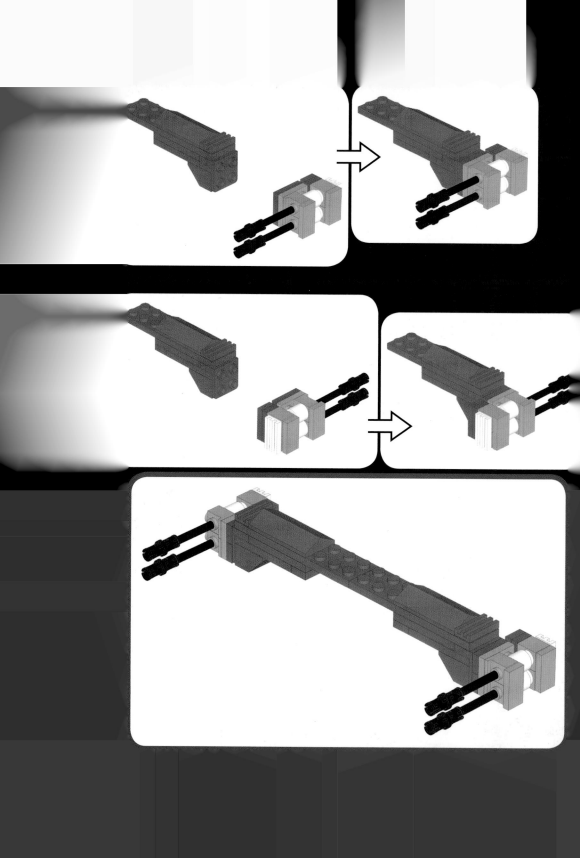

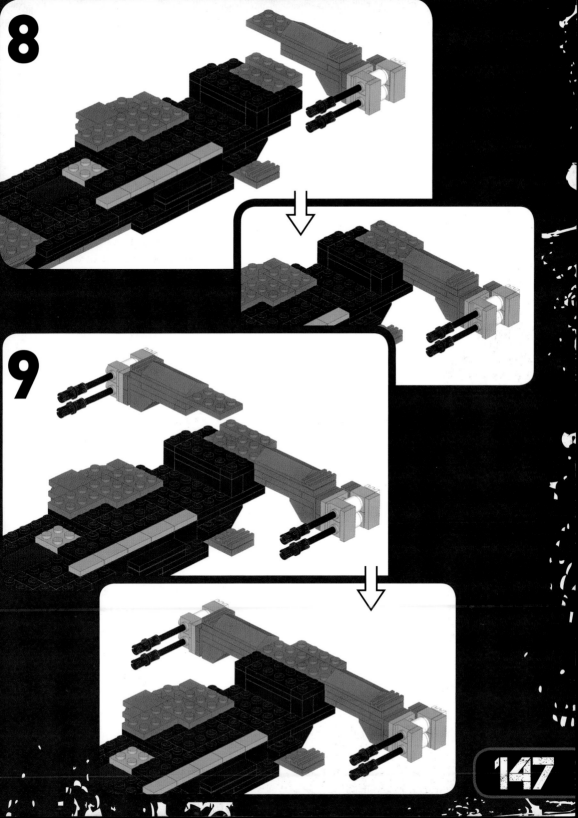

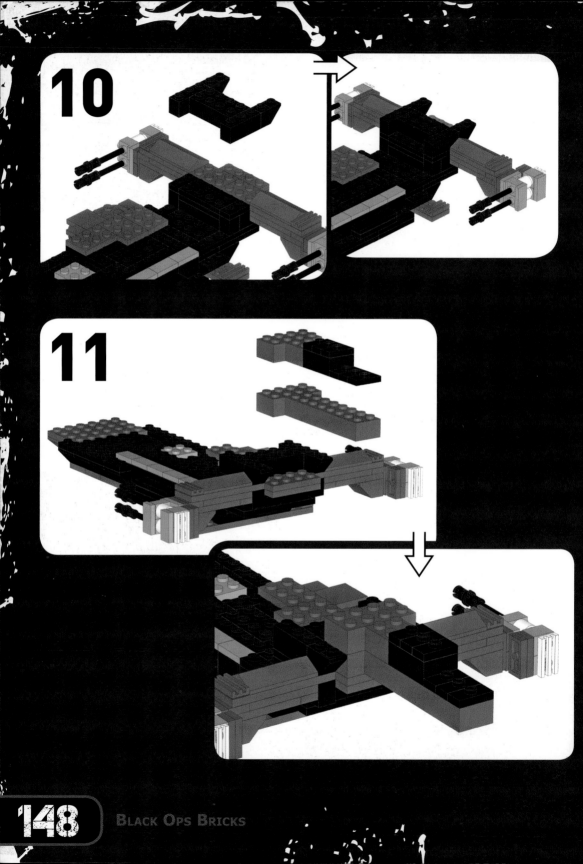

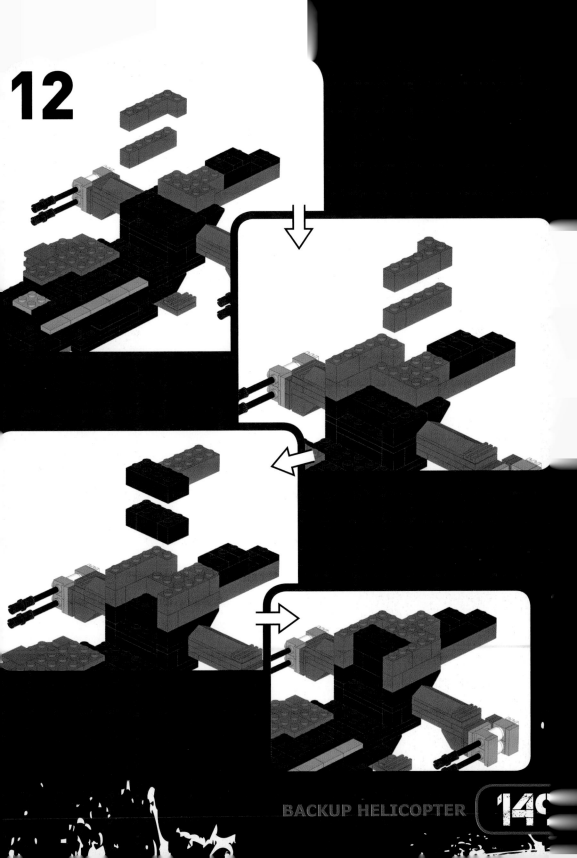

12

13

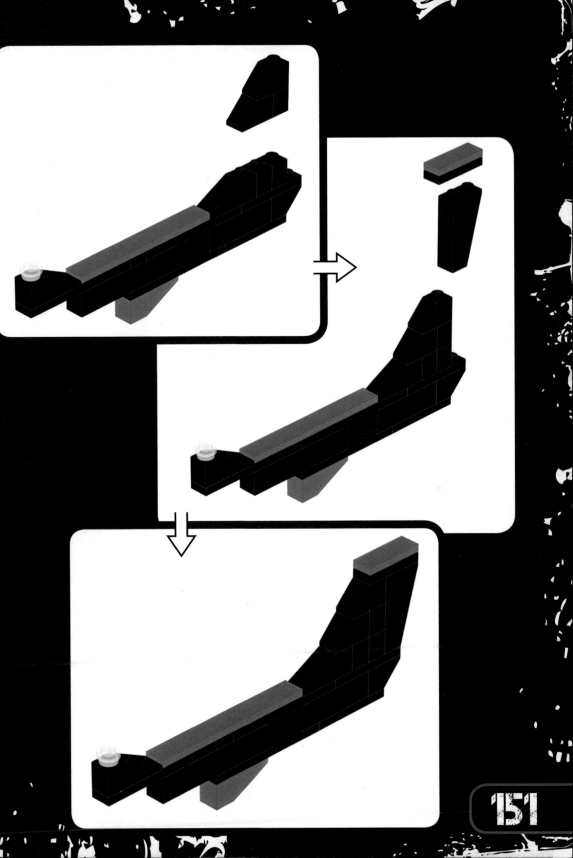

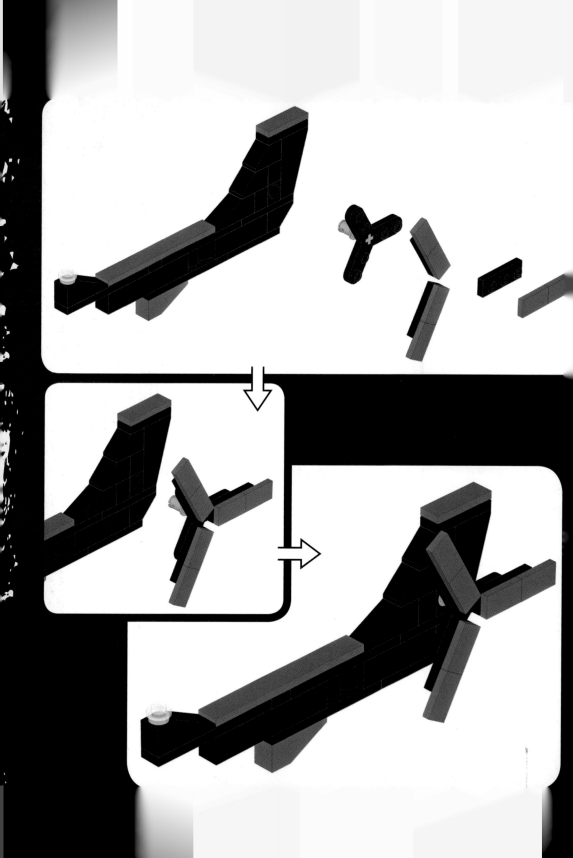

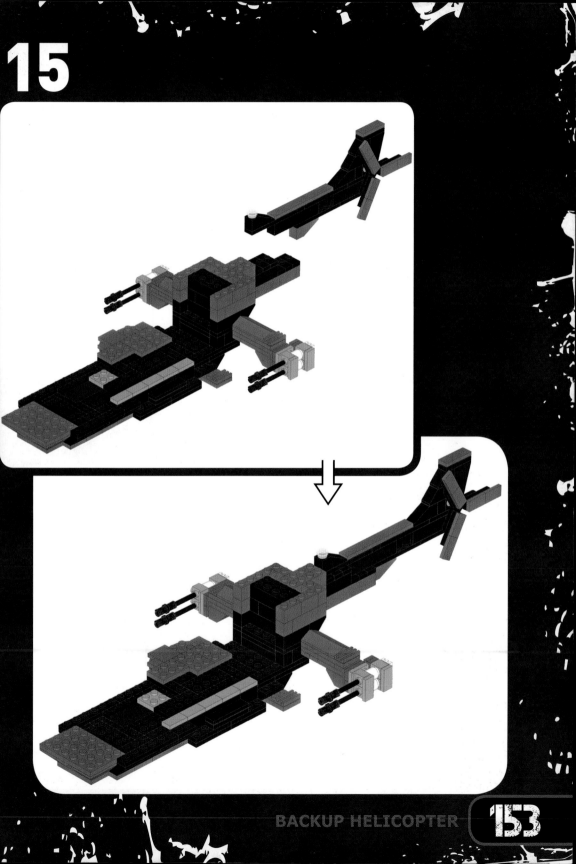

15

BACKUP HELICOPTER

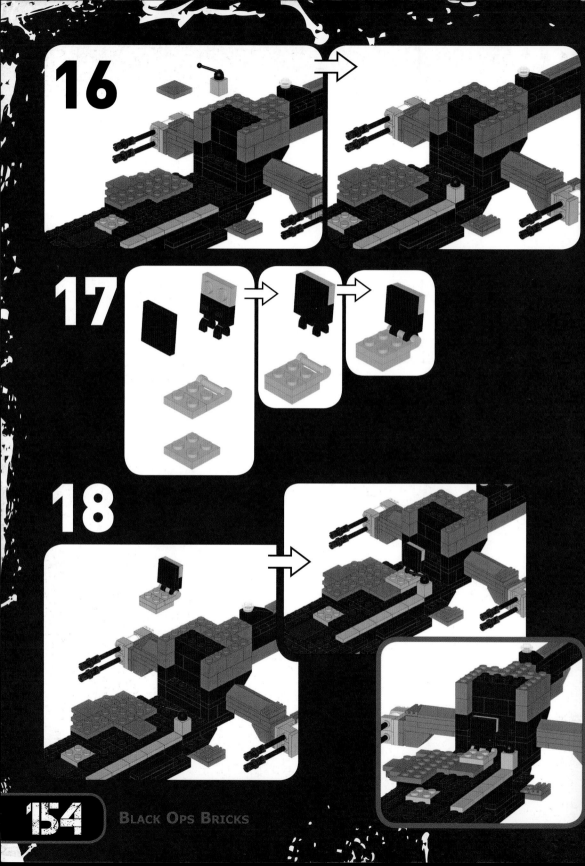

16

17

18

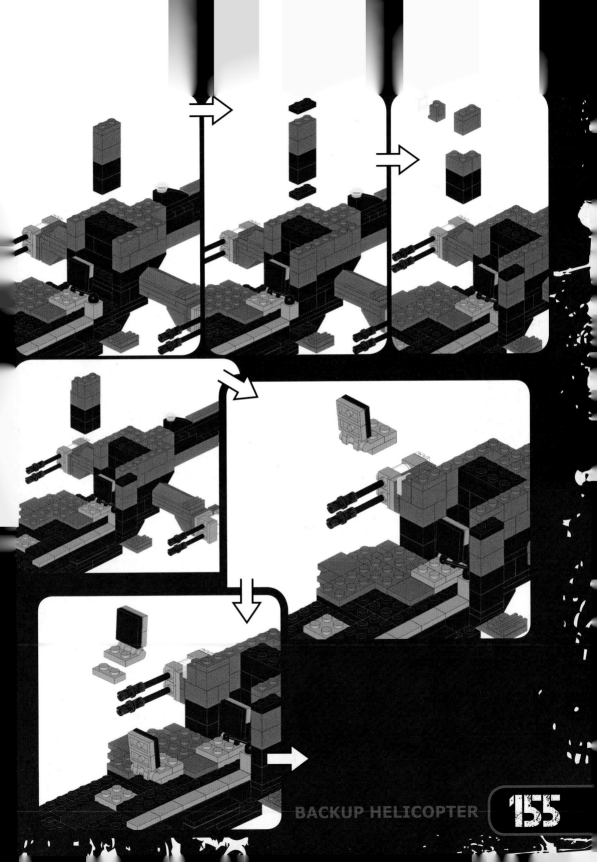

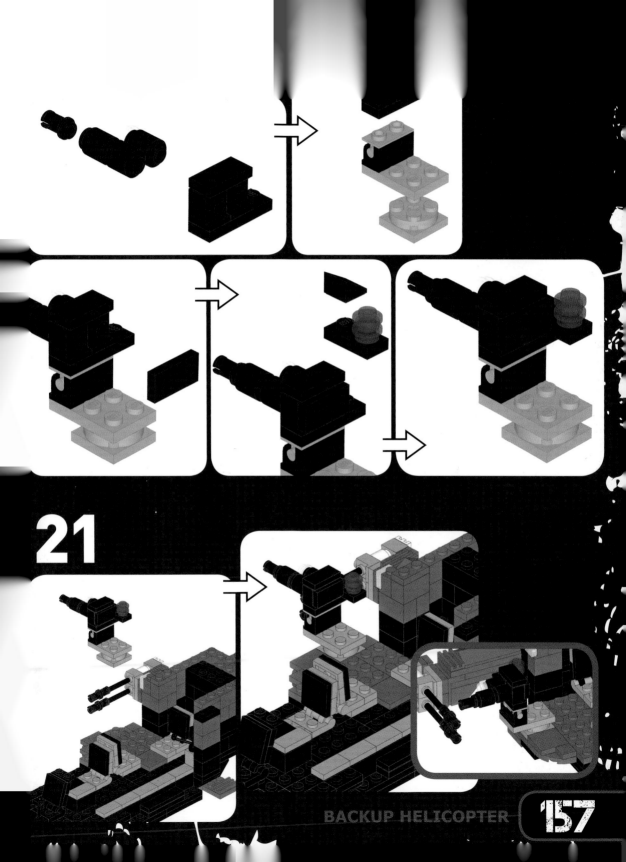

21

22

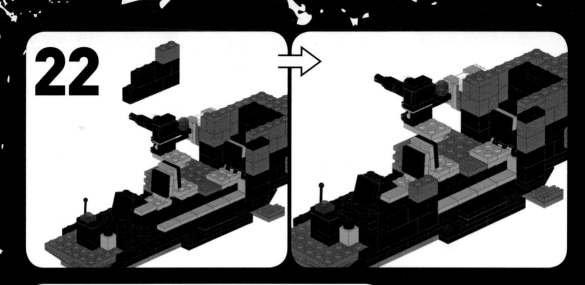

23

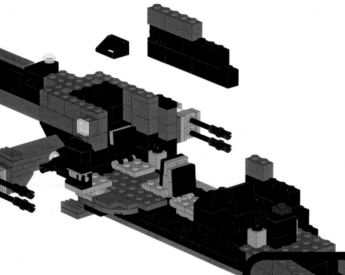

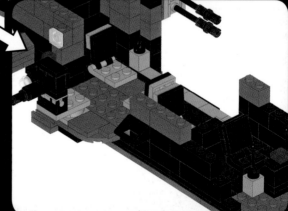

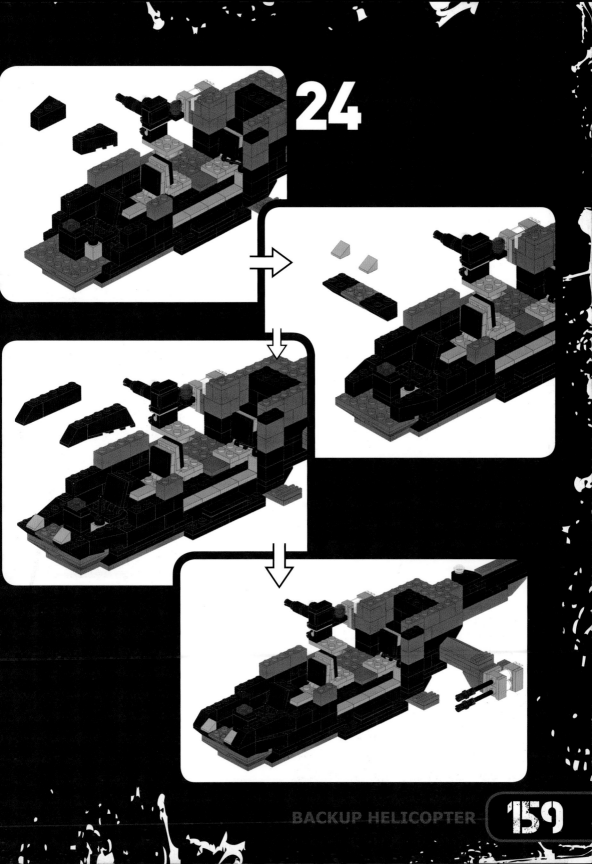

24

25

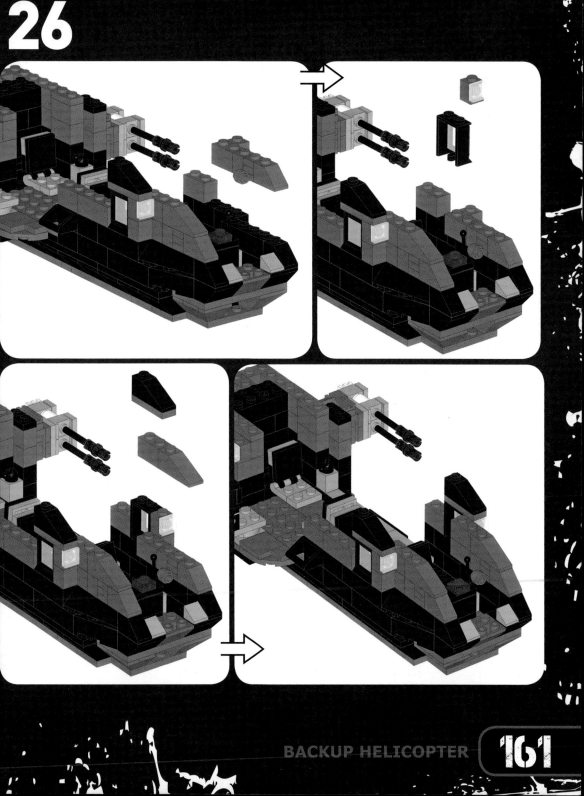

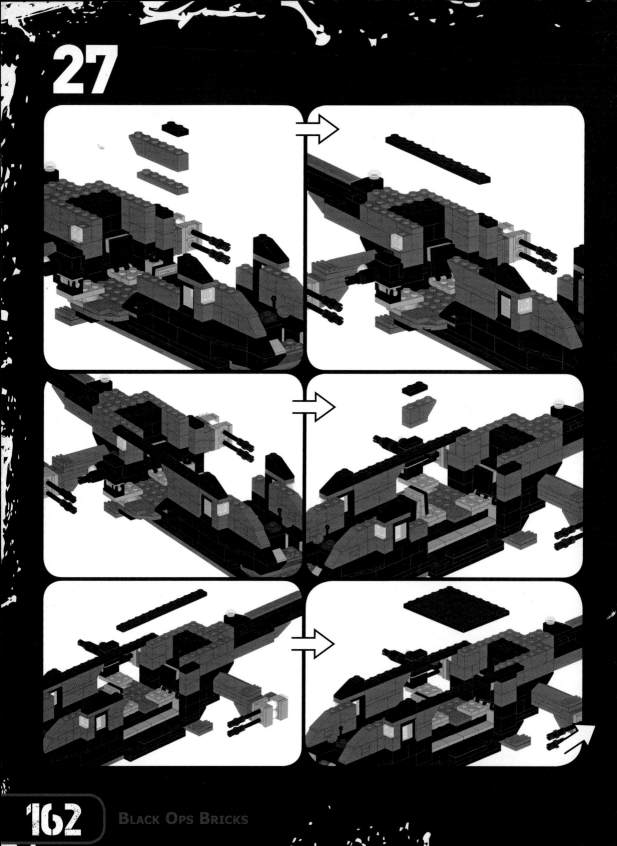

BLACK OPS BRICKS

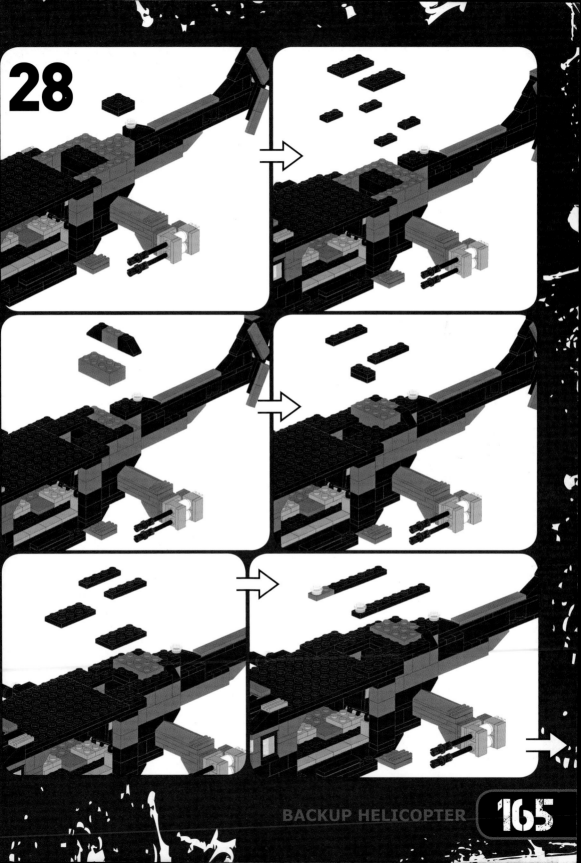

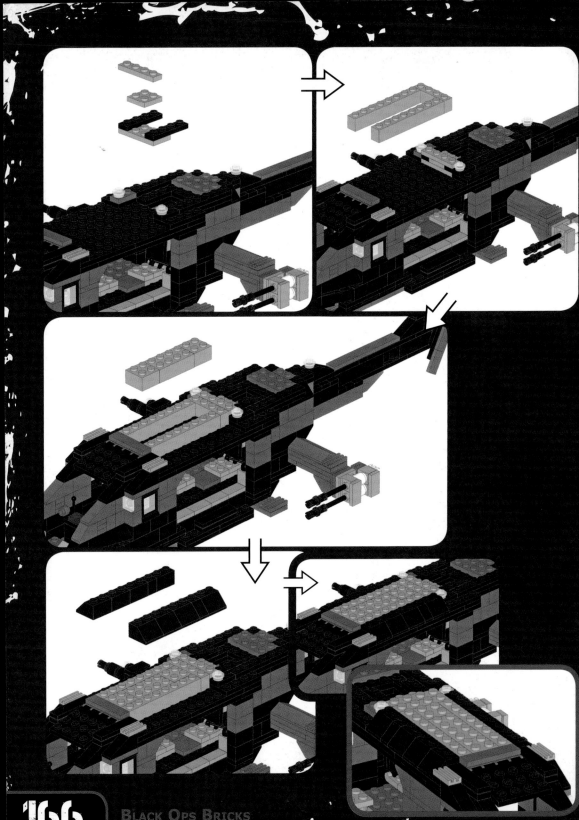

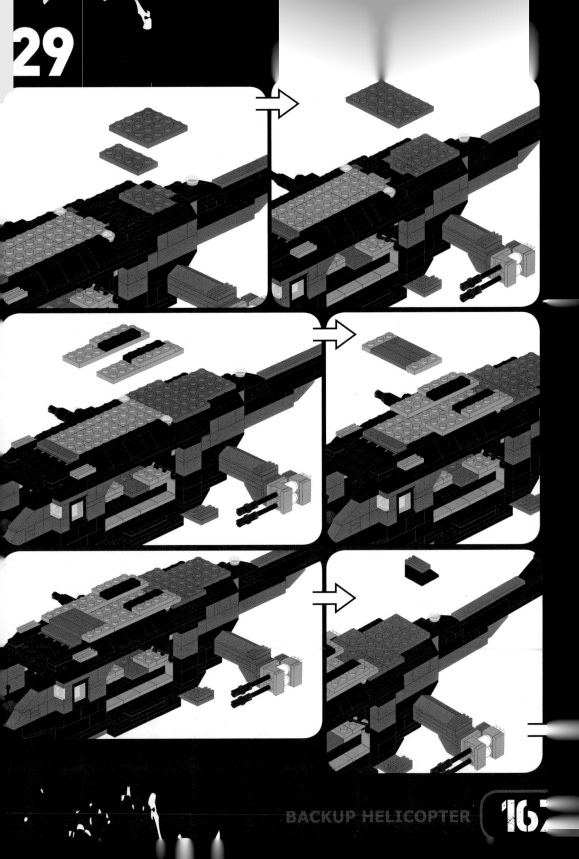

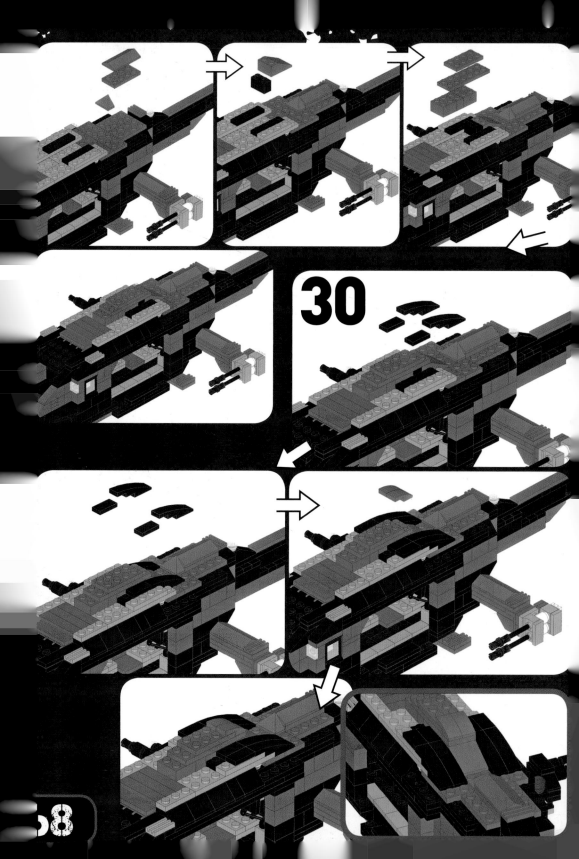

30

31

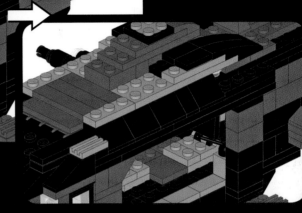

32

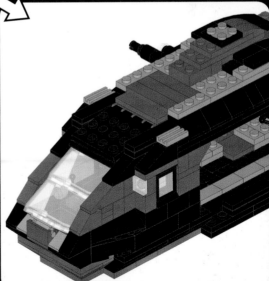

33

34

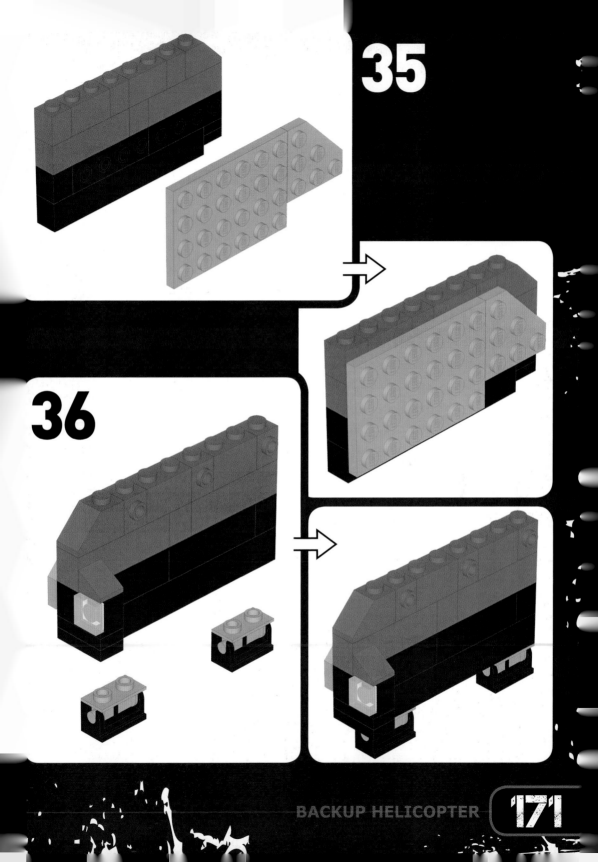

35

36

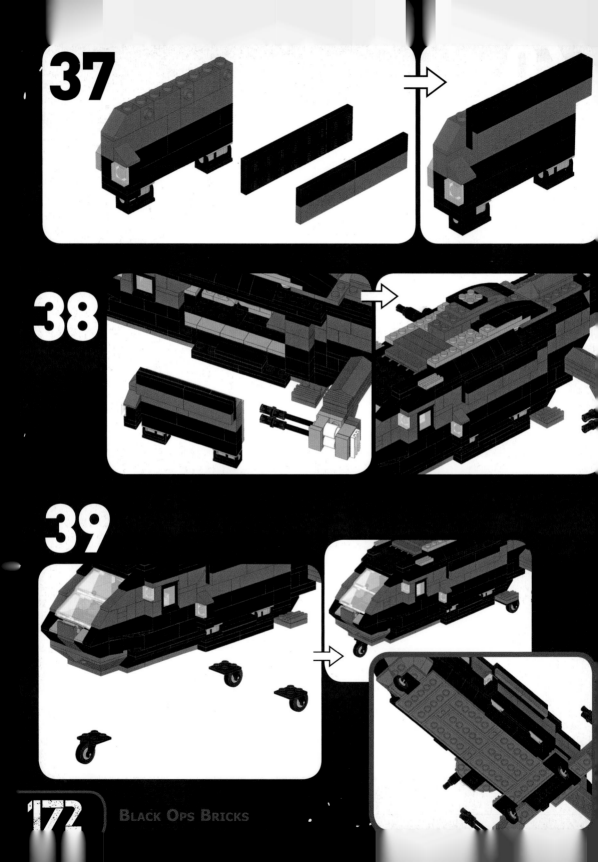

37

38

39

40

4x

41

42

4x

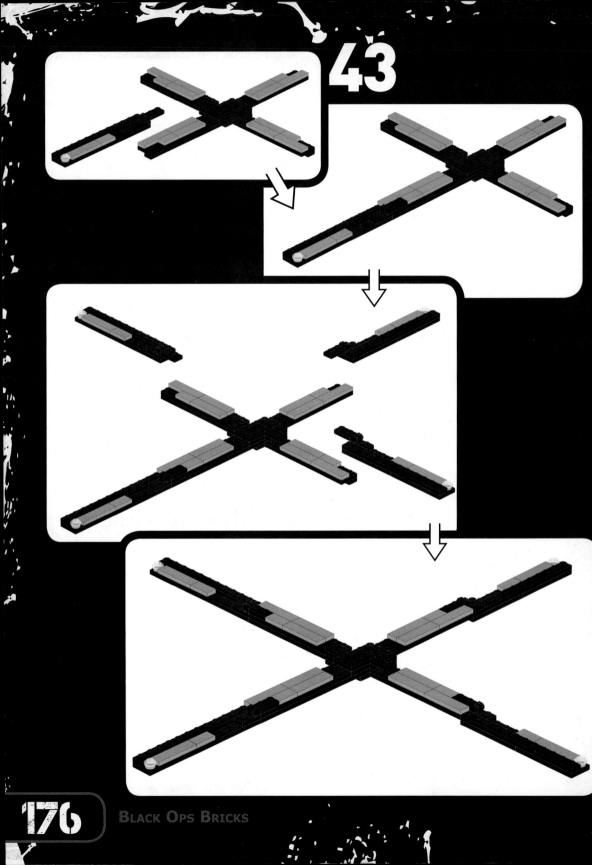

43

44

45

Done

MOBILE MISSLE BATTERY

PIECE COUNT:
- 179 elements

FEATURES:
- Rotating control tower
- Rotating salvo-style
missile launcher

When something needs to be guarded, this is what you use. This vehicle can launch missiles, smoke grenades, and napalm at extreme distances.

The two-man team that operates this can take their roaming sentry tower anywhere and still have a 360 degree view of the battle.

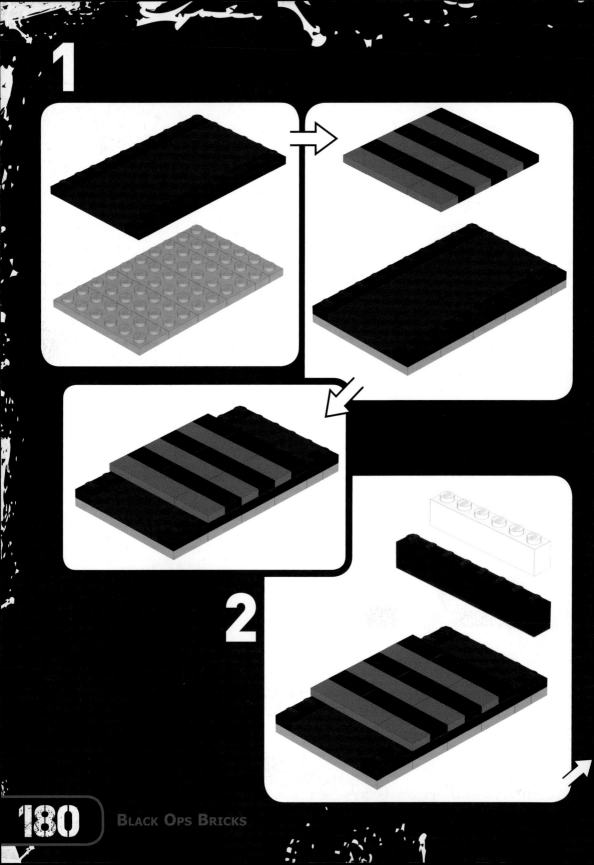

1

2

BLACK OPS BRICKS

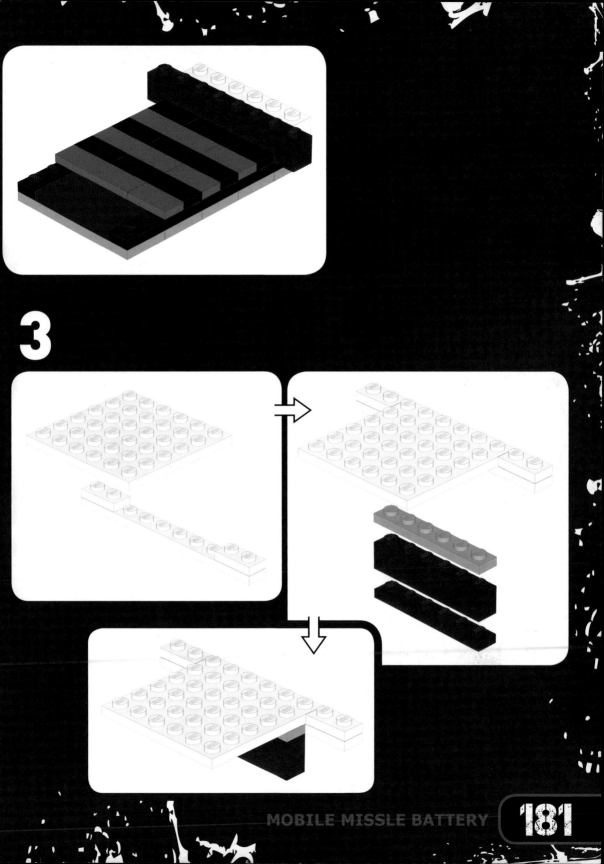

3

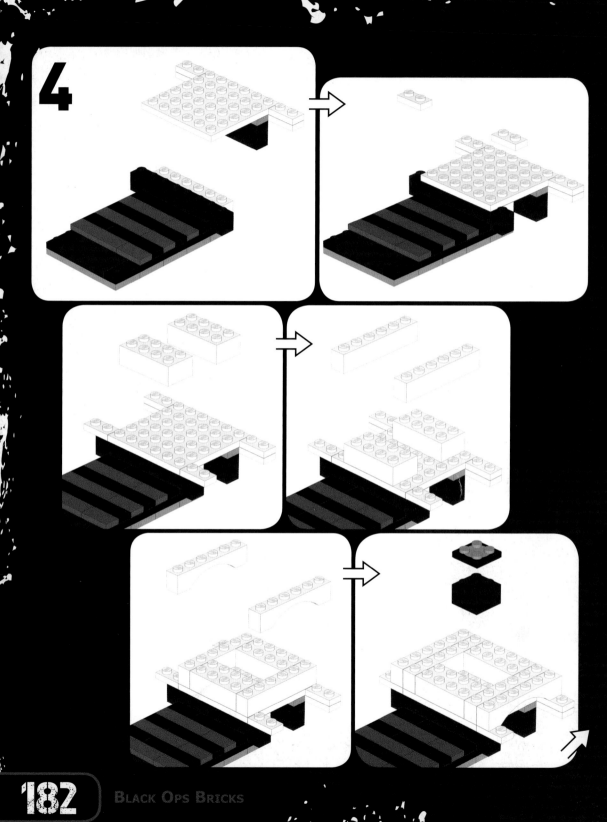

BLACK OPS BRICKS

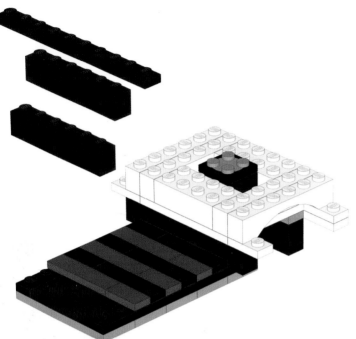

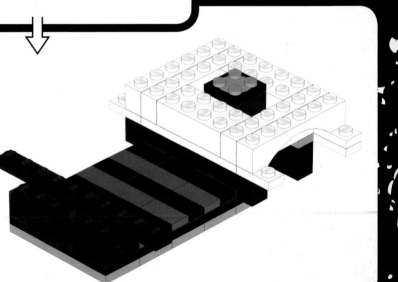

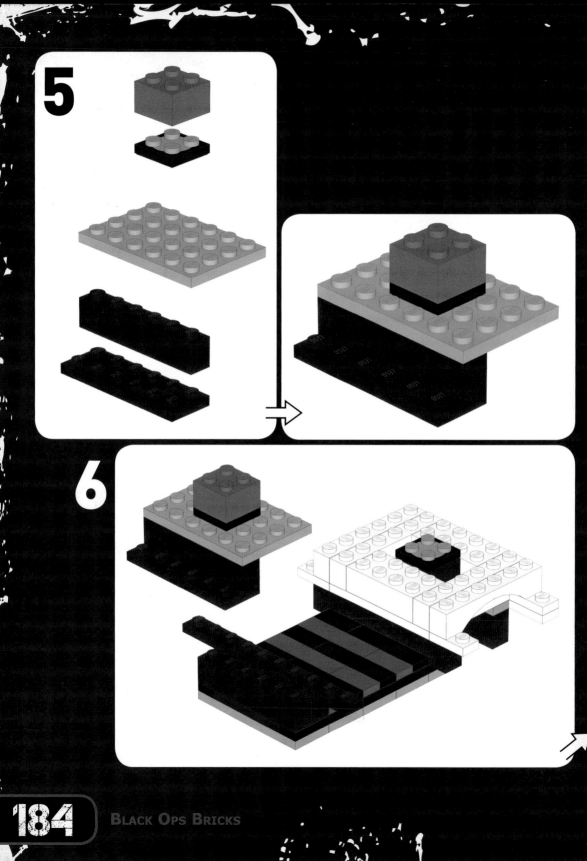

5

6

BLACK OPS BRICKS

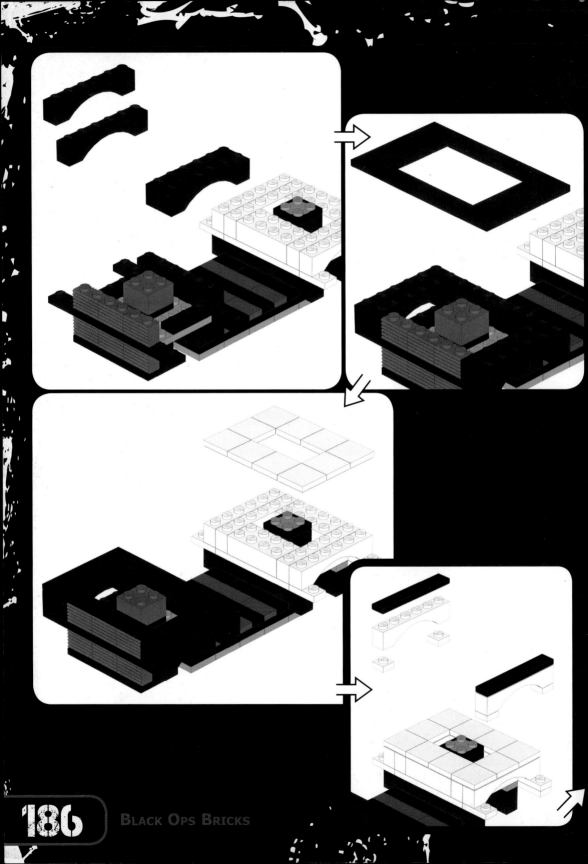

BLACK OPS BRICKS

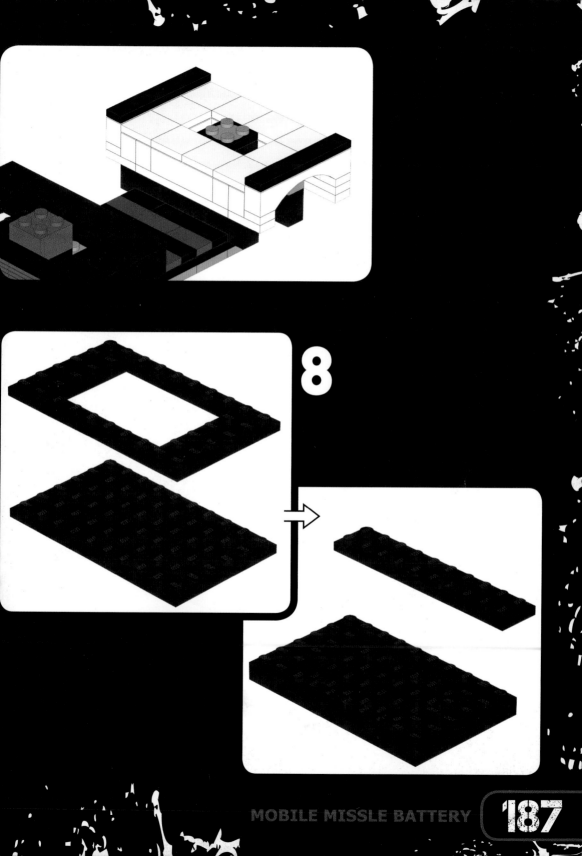

8

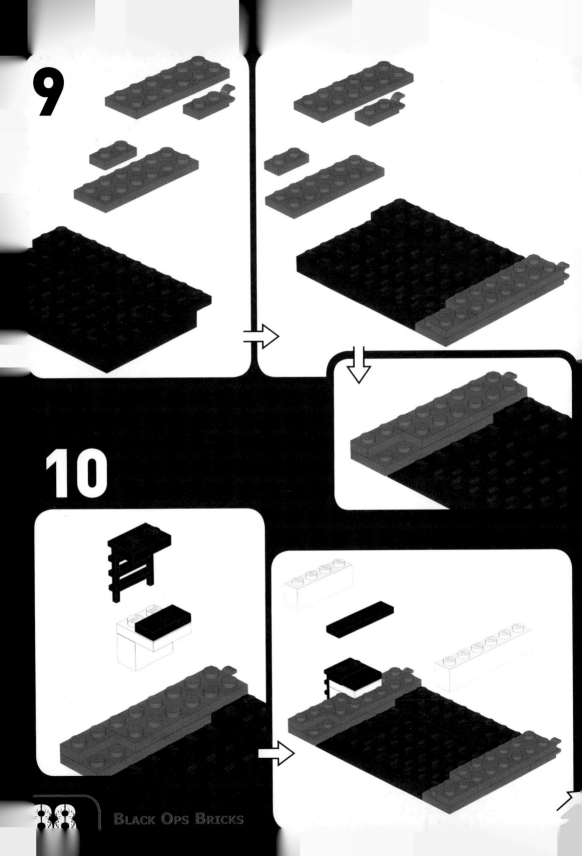

9

10

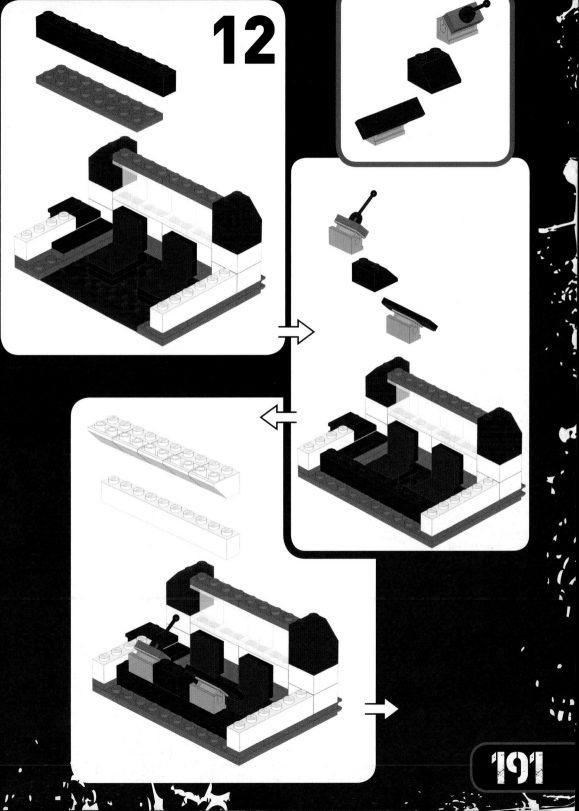

13

BLACK OPS BRICKS

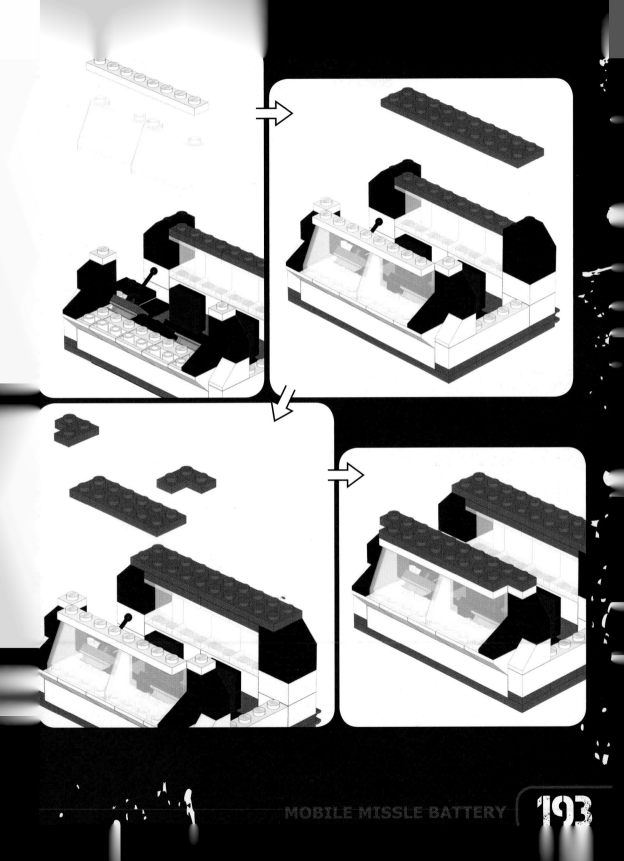

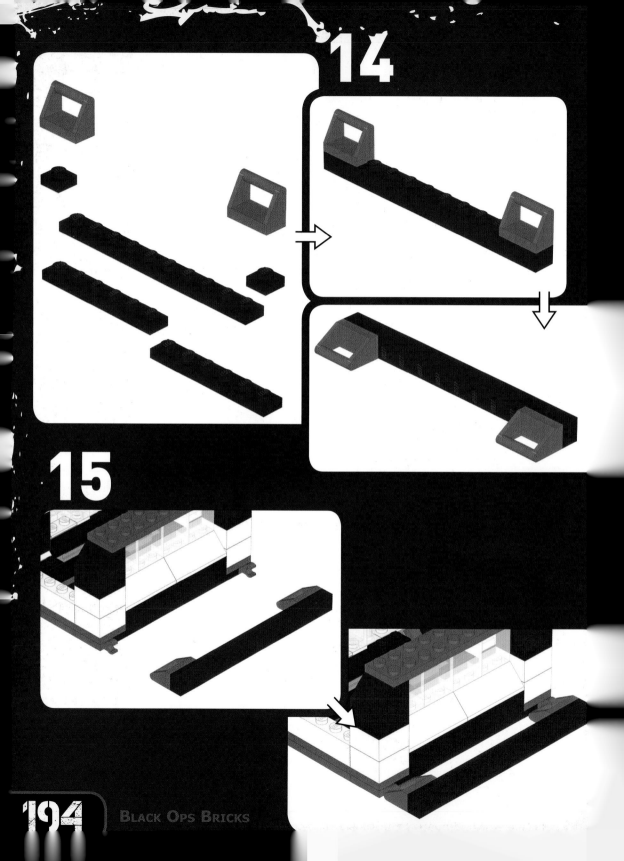

14

15

BLACK OPS BRICKS

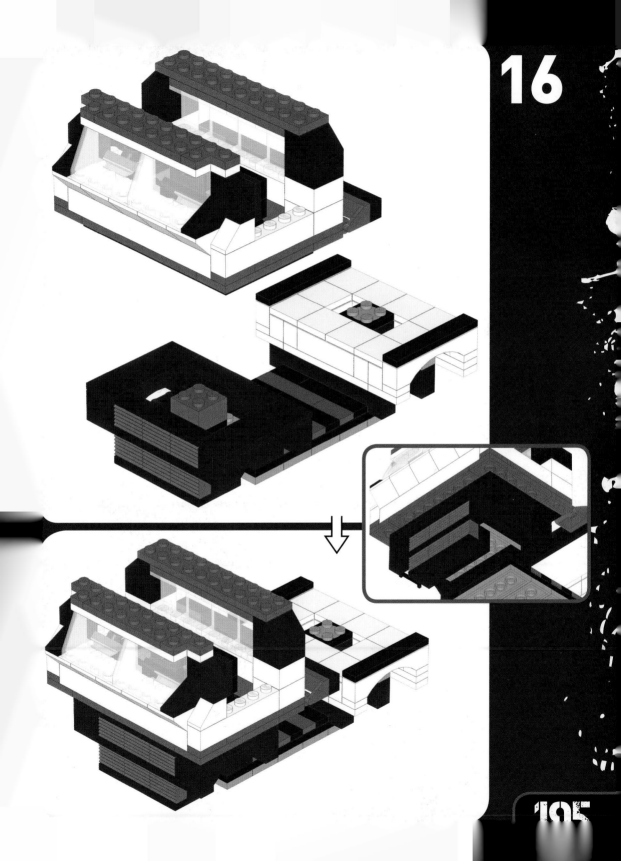

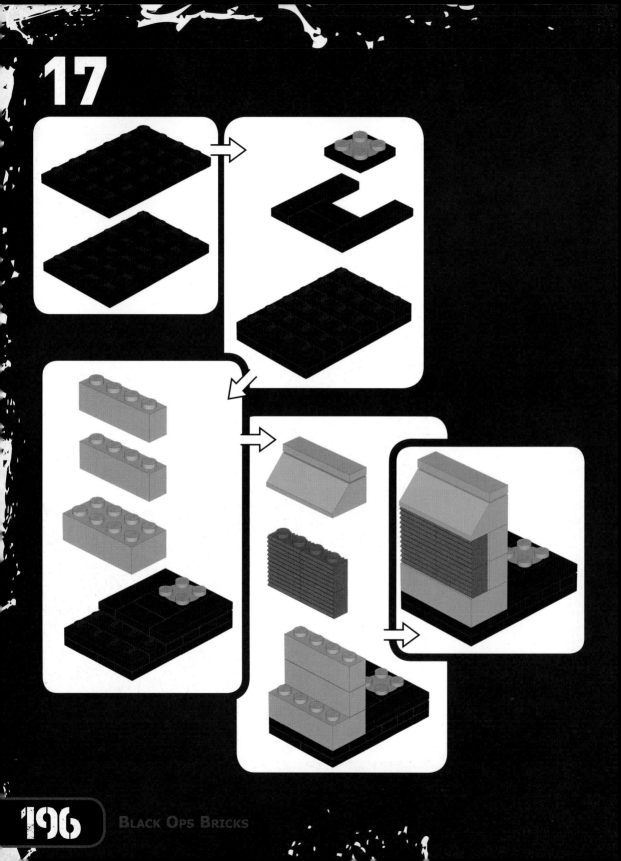

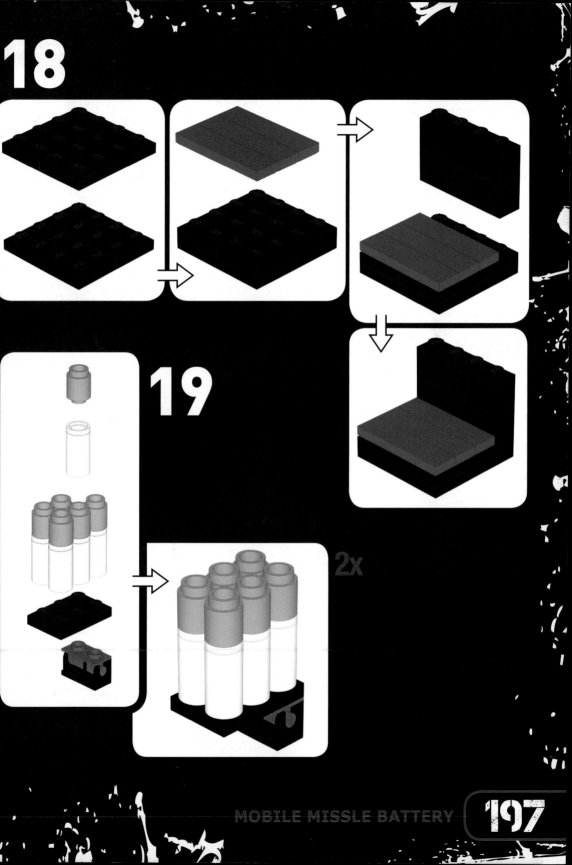

18

19

2x

20

21

22

23

2x

24

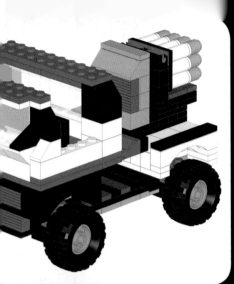
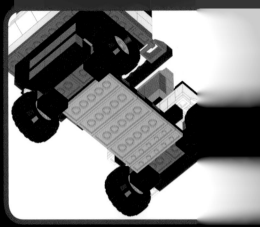

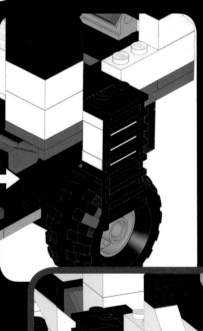

Done

VTOL FIGHTER JET

PIECE COUNT:

- 576 elements

FEATURES:

- Fold-out machine guns
- Enclosed navigator seat behind the pilot
- Vertical take-off and landing capabilities.

Rumor has it that the military scrapped their entire fleet of jets to replace it with these.

This thing has missiles galore, hidden machine guns, and a secondary emergency pilot seat. This jet rules the skies with its crazy acrobatic capabilities and dangerous weapon load-out.

1

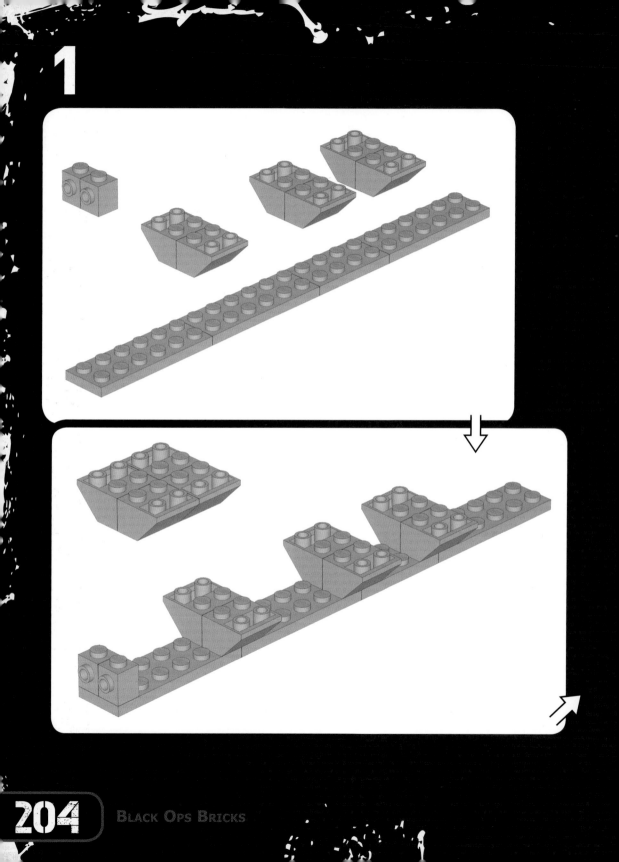

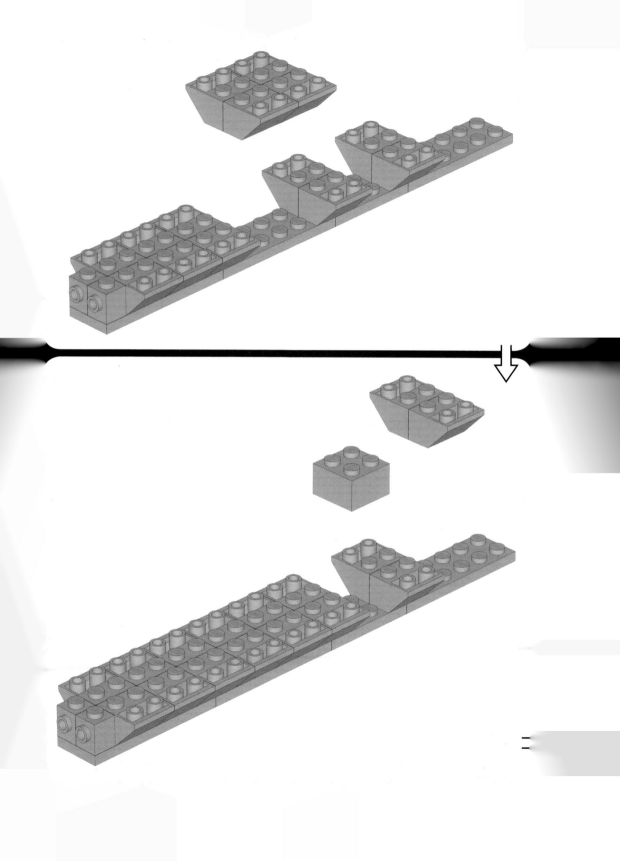

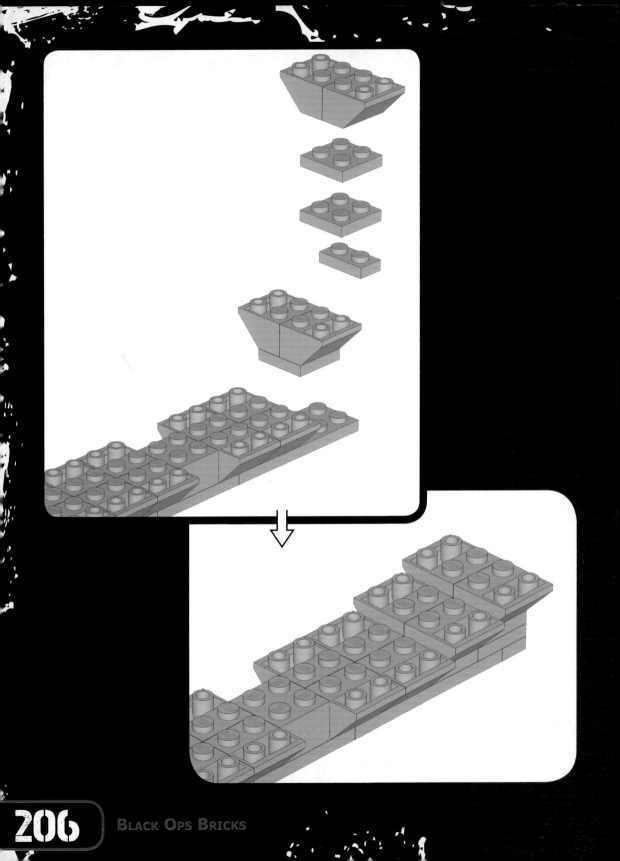

BLACK OPS BRICKS

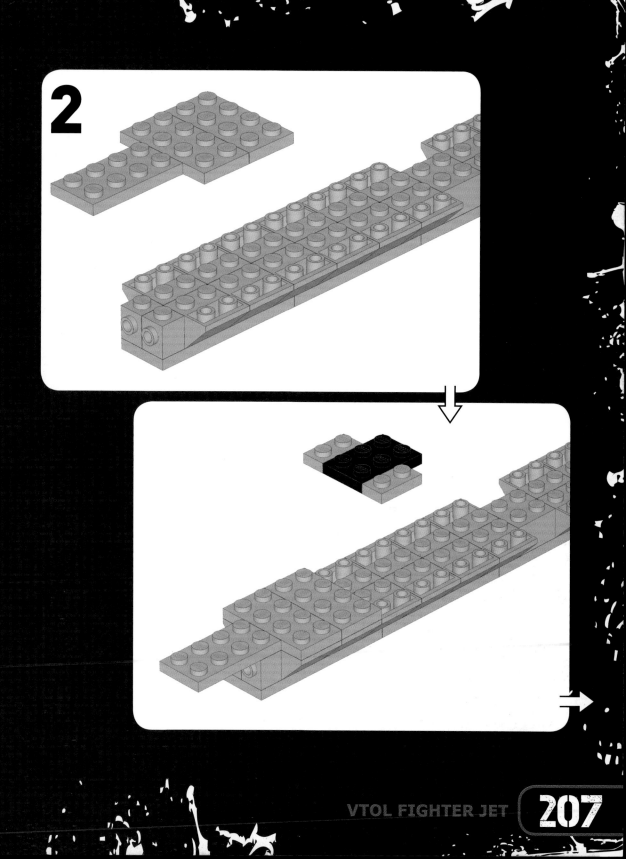

2

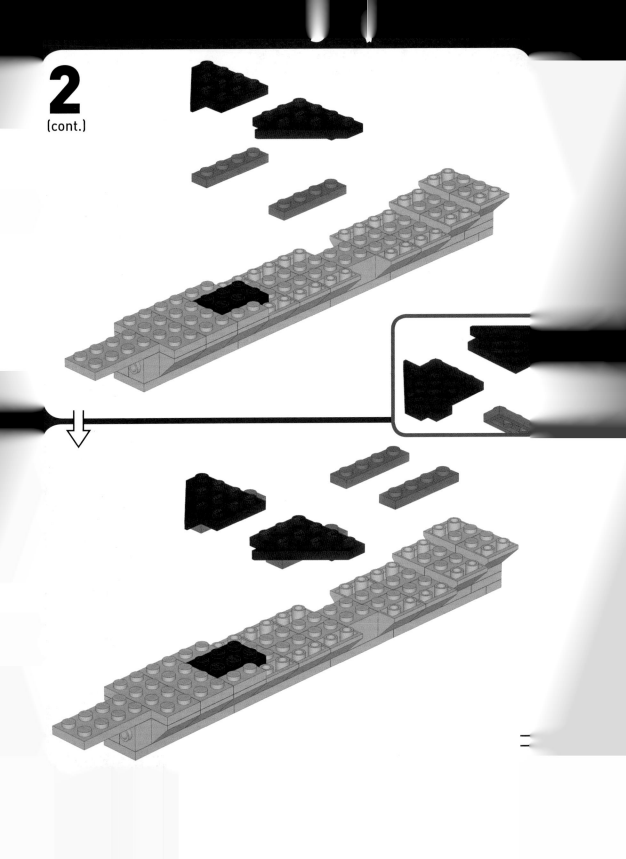

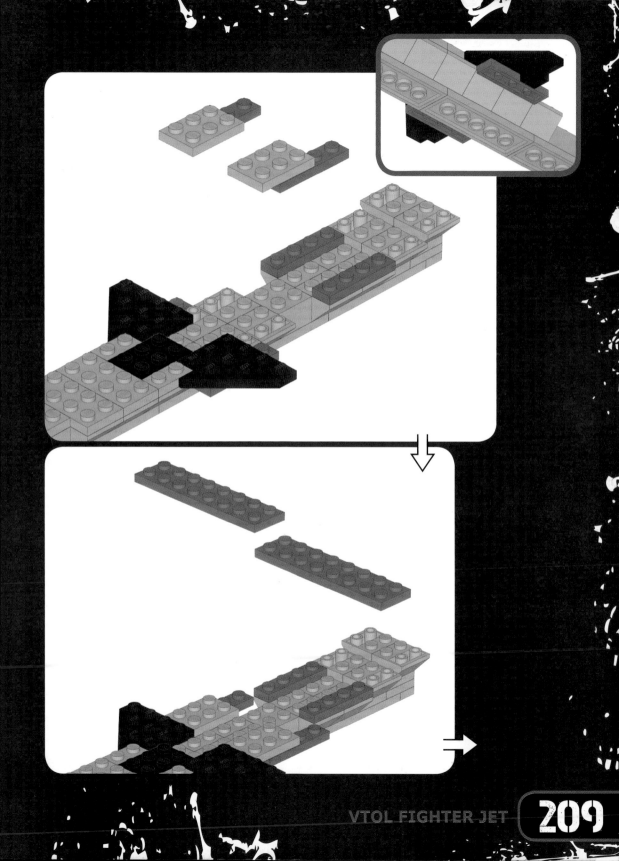

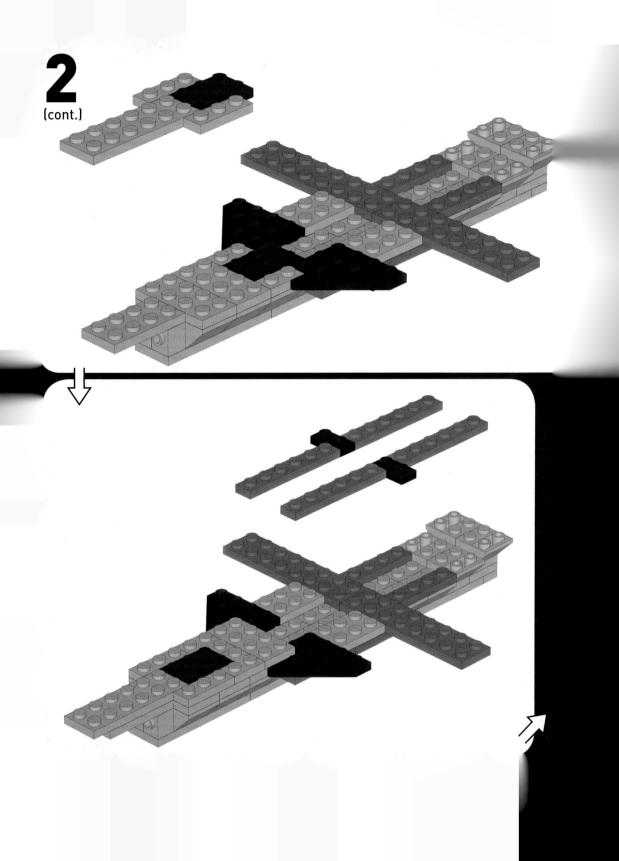

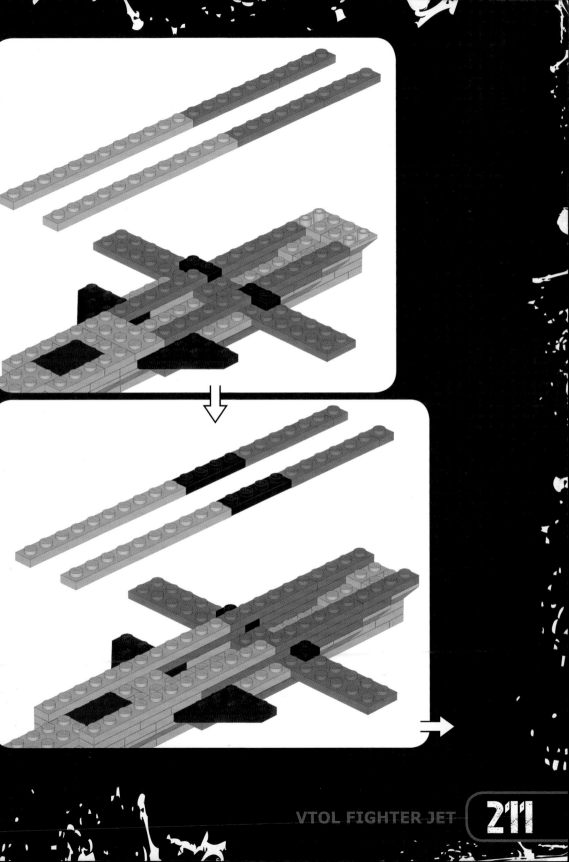

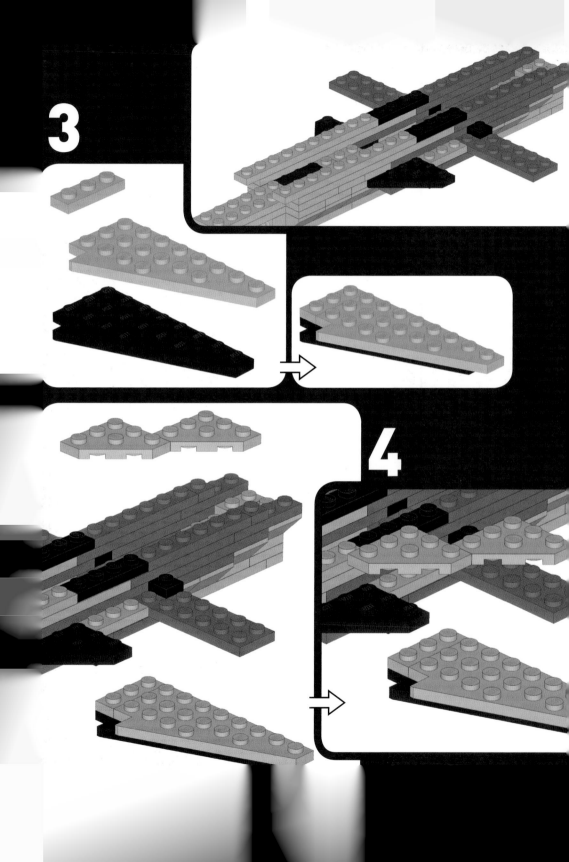

5

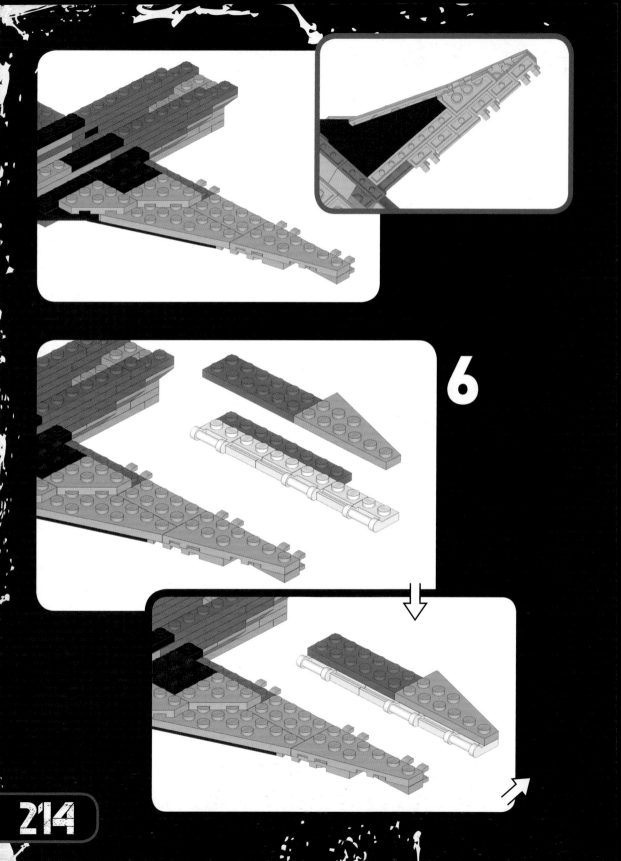

6

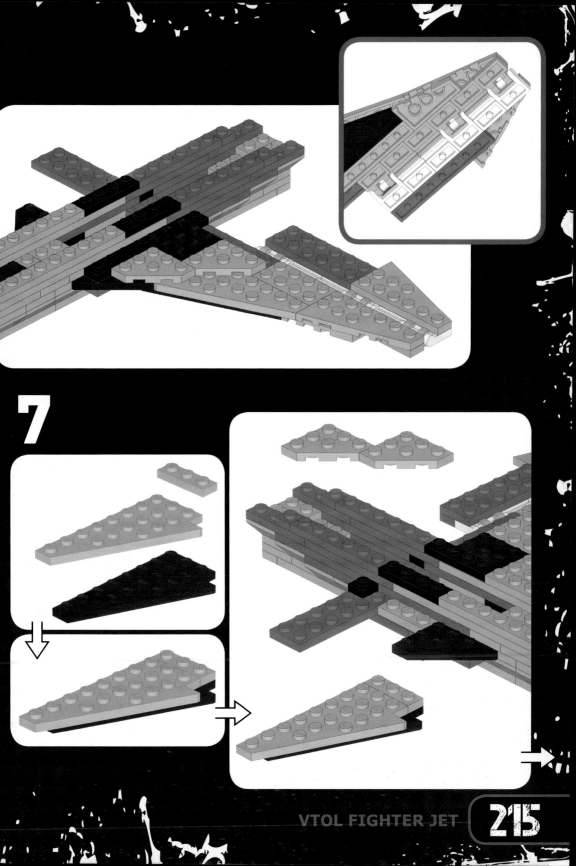

7

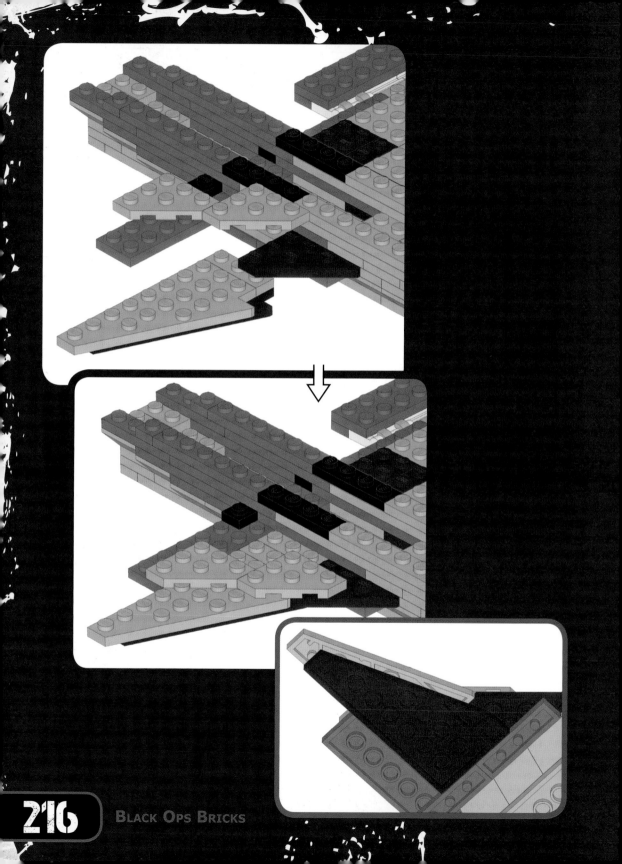

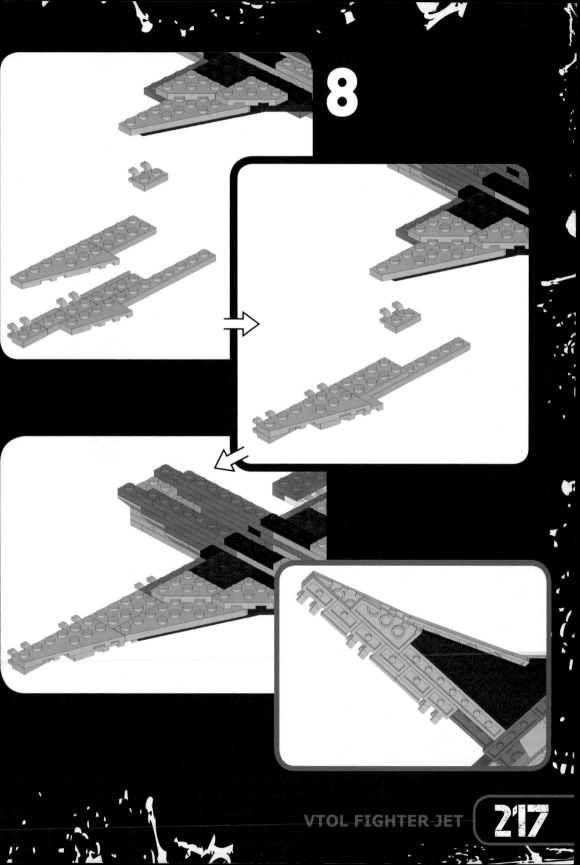

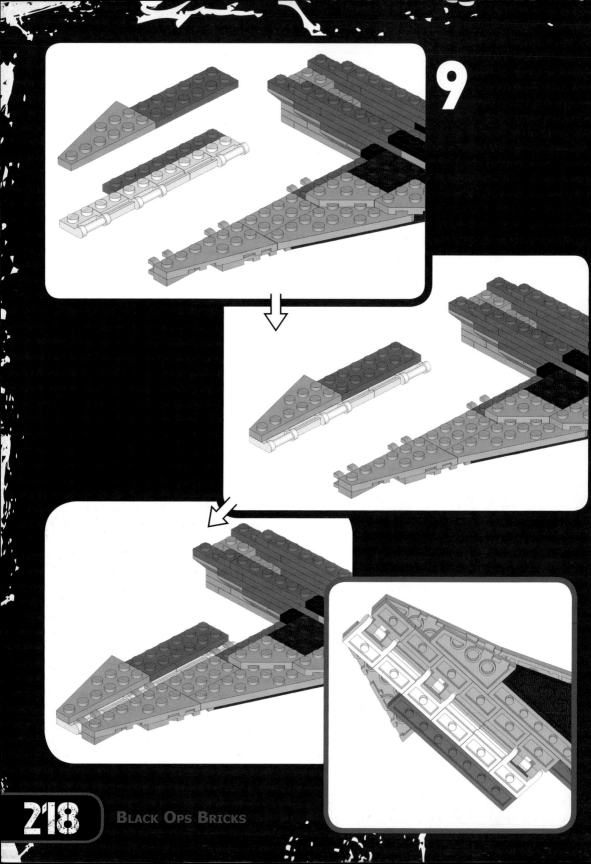

9

BLACK OPS BRICKS

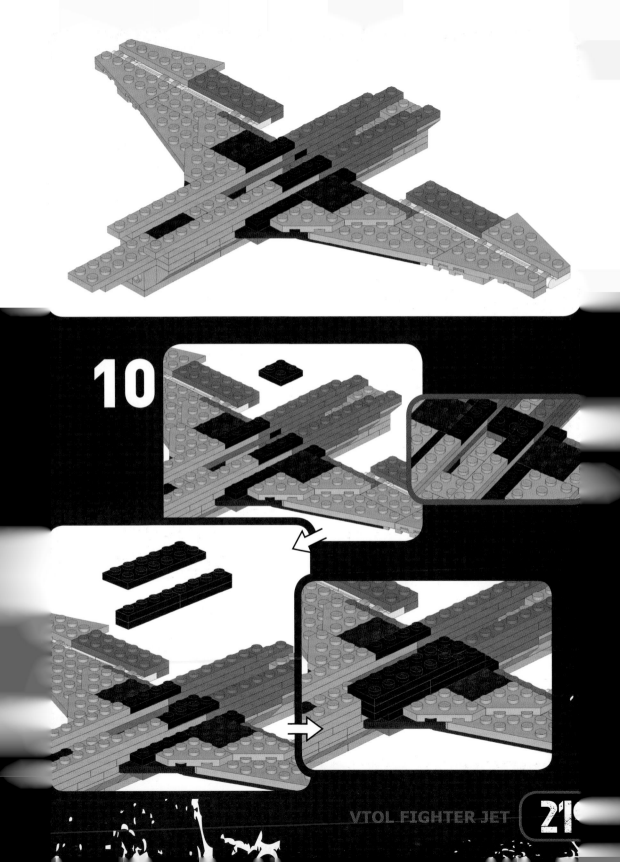

10

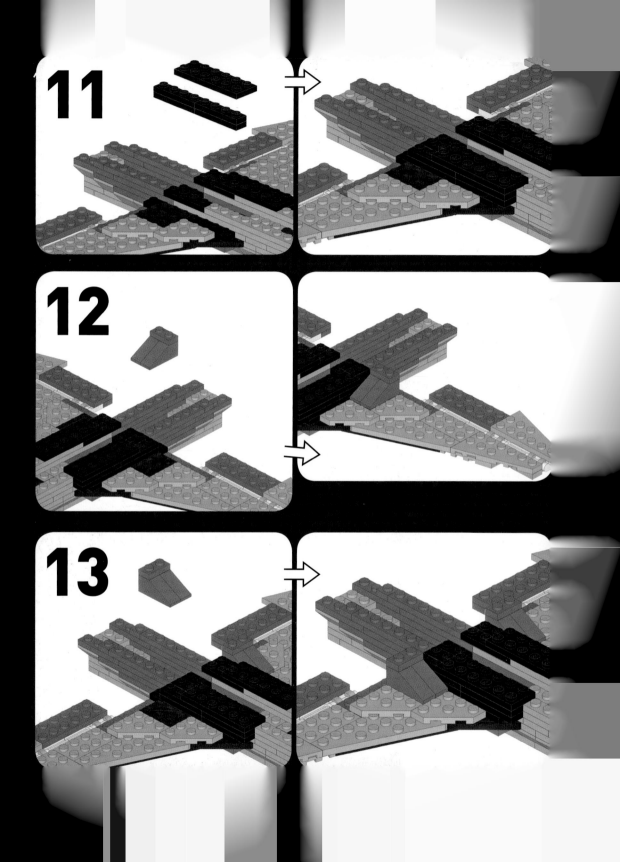

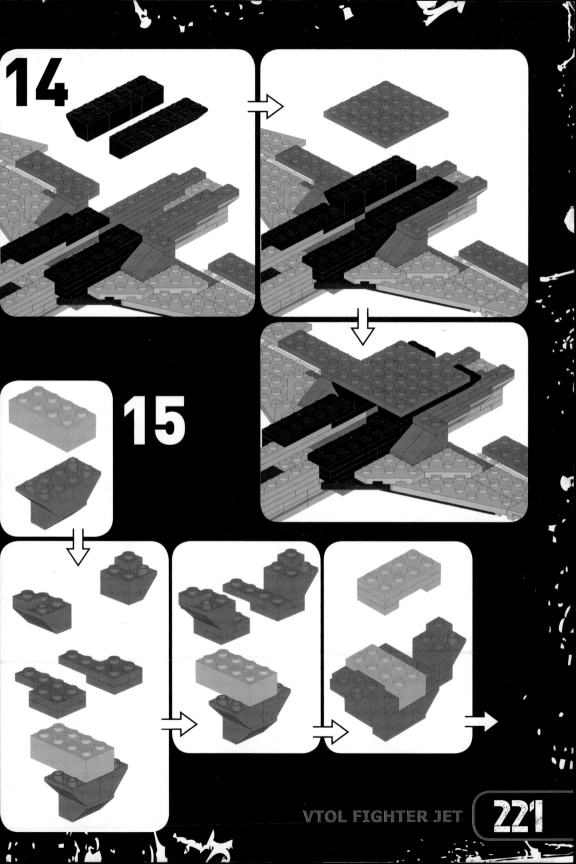

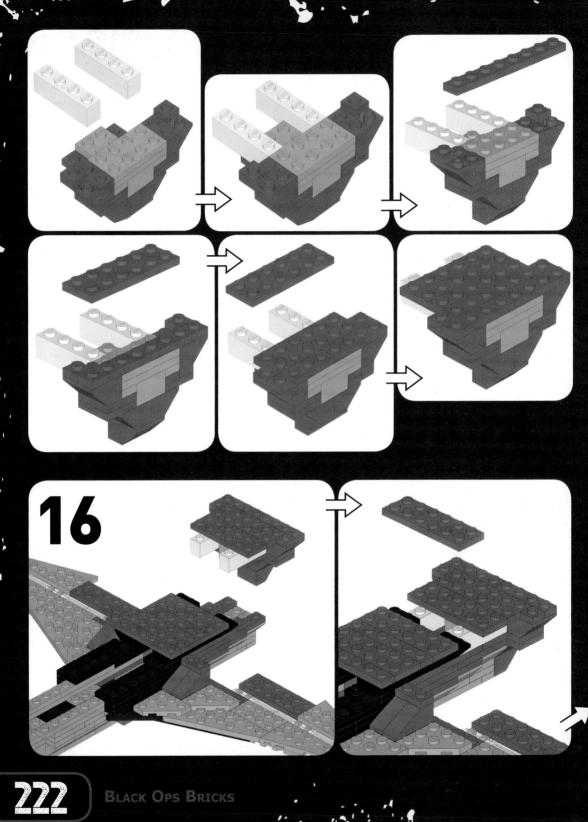

16

BLACK OPS BRICKS

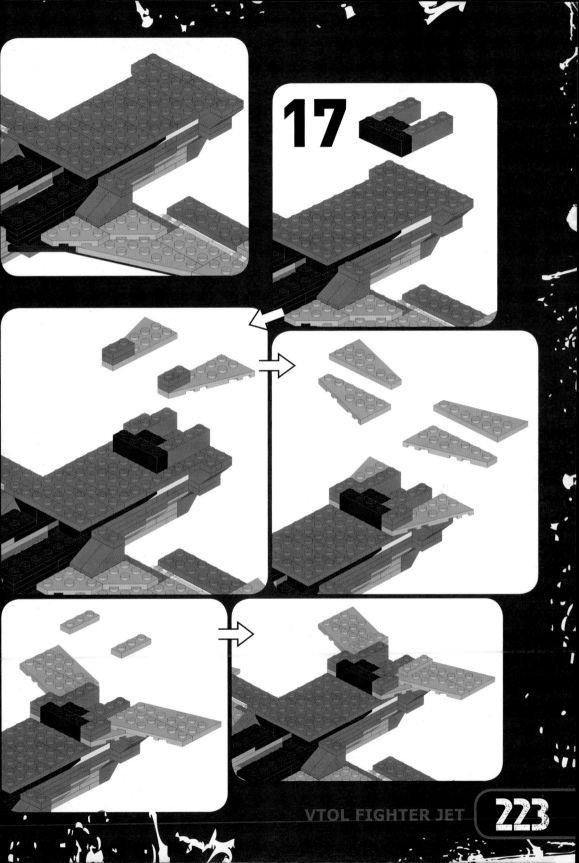

17

18

19

20

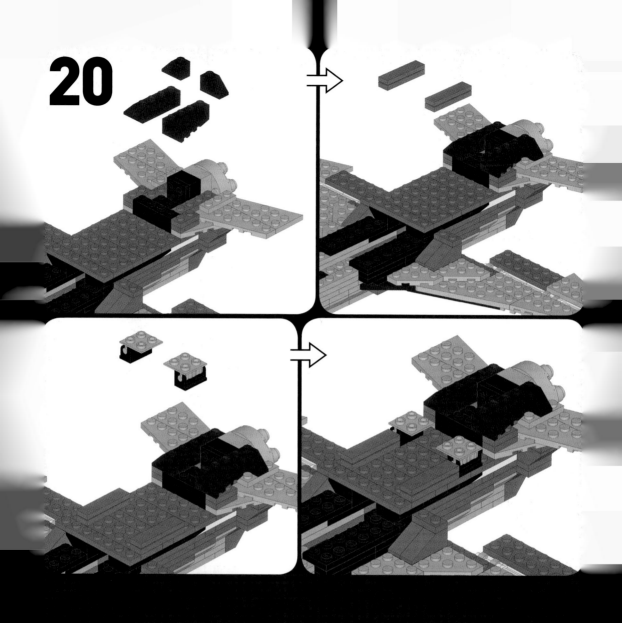

21

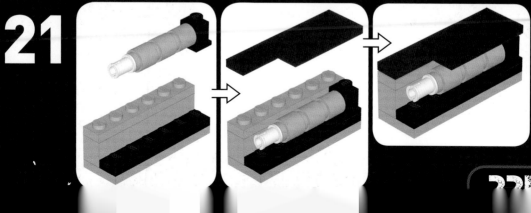

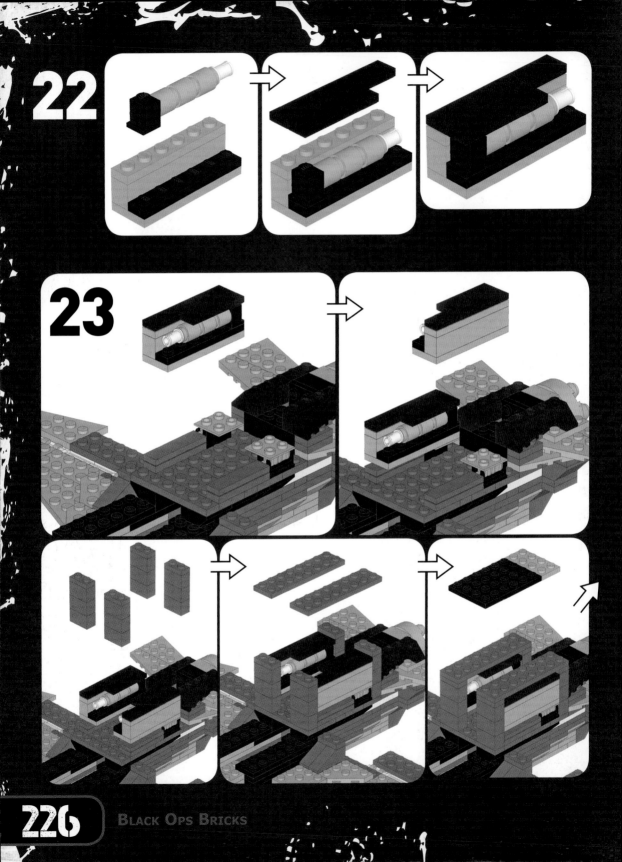

22

23

BLACK OPS BRICKS

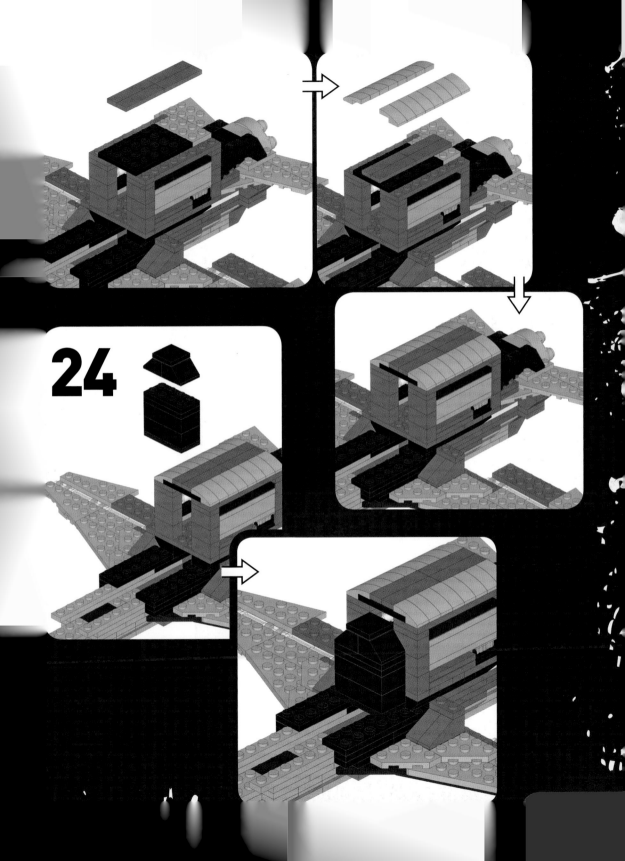

24

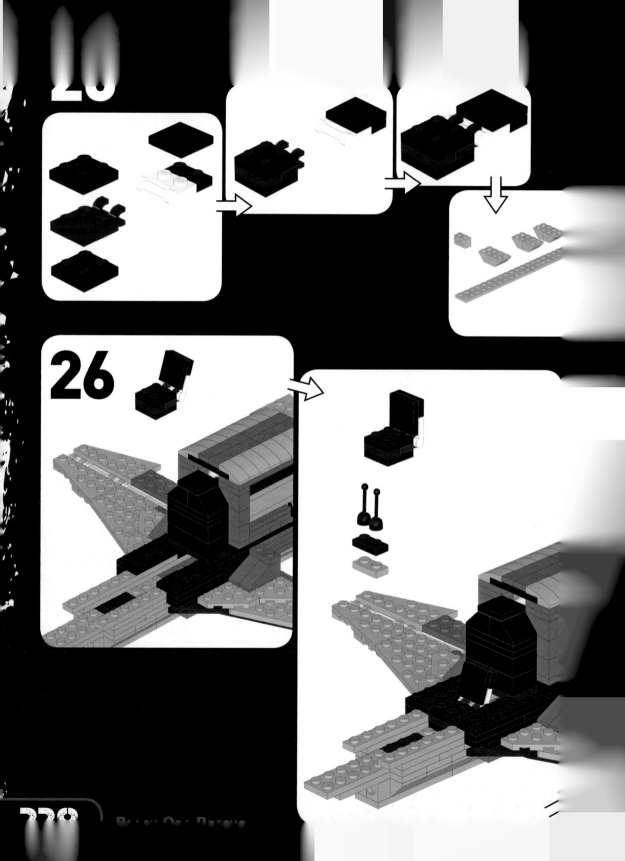

26

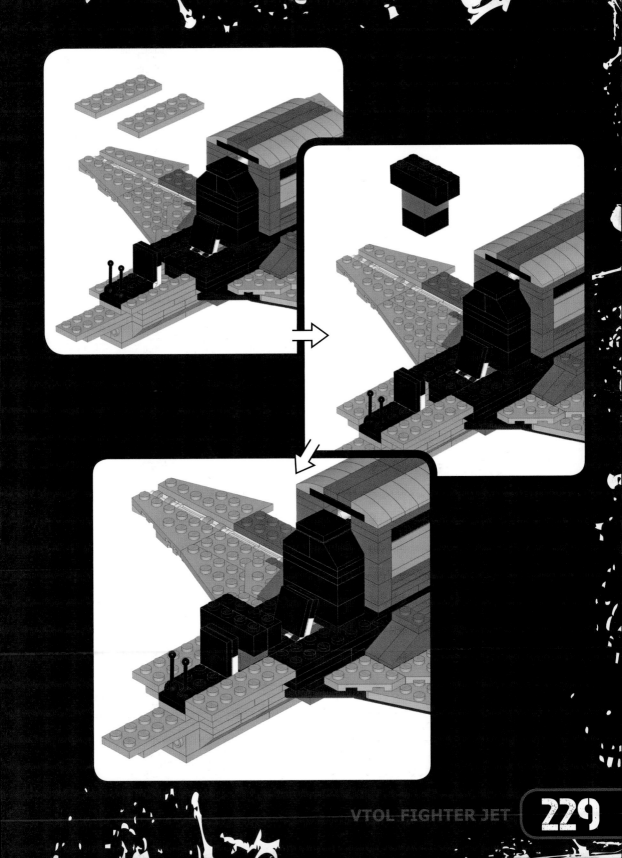

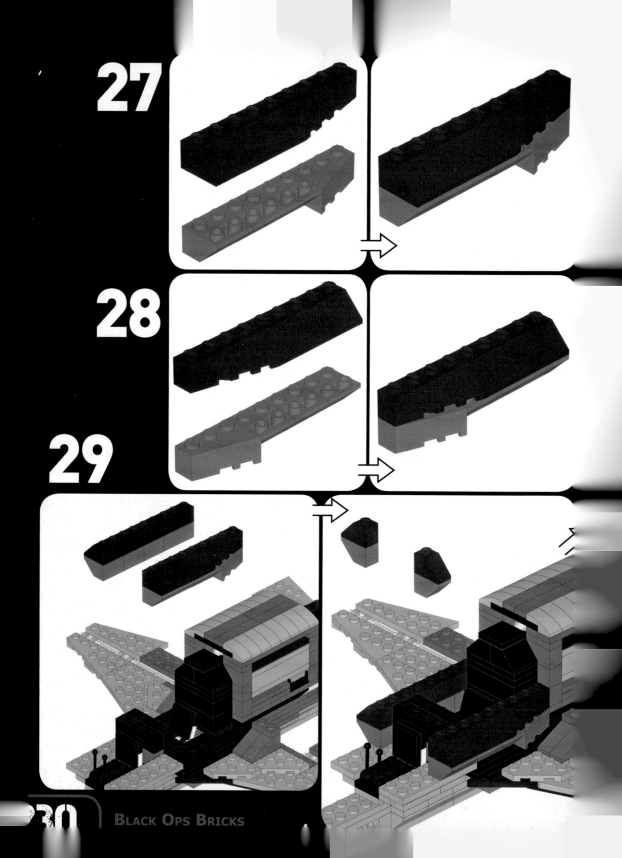

27

28

29

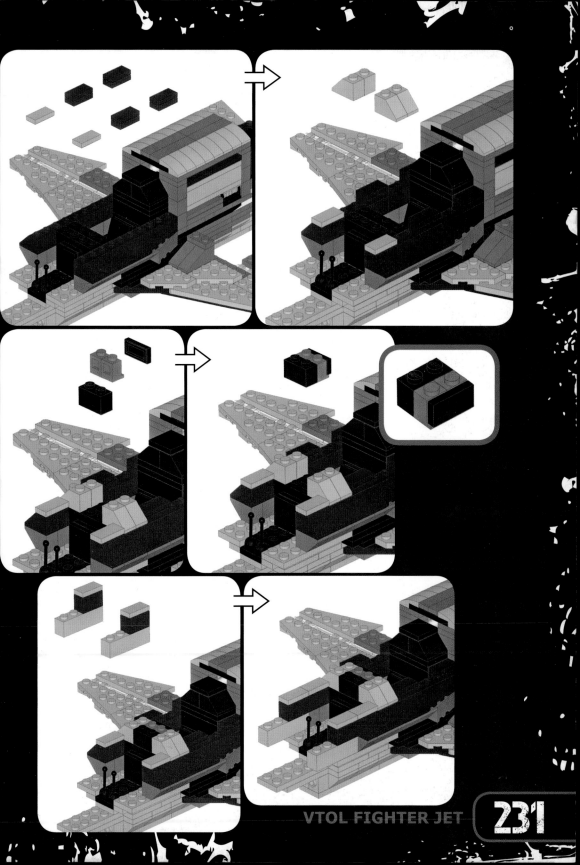

30

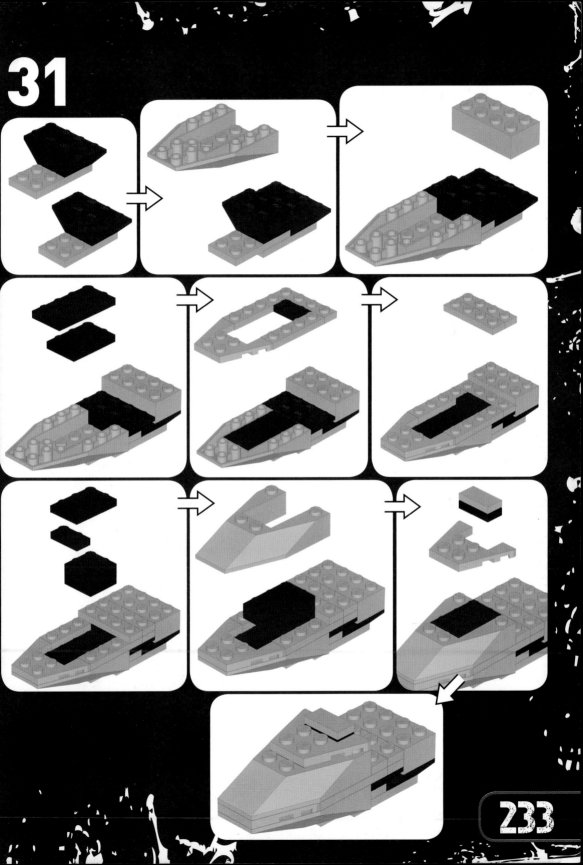

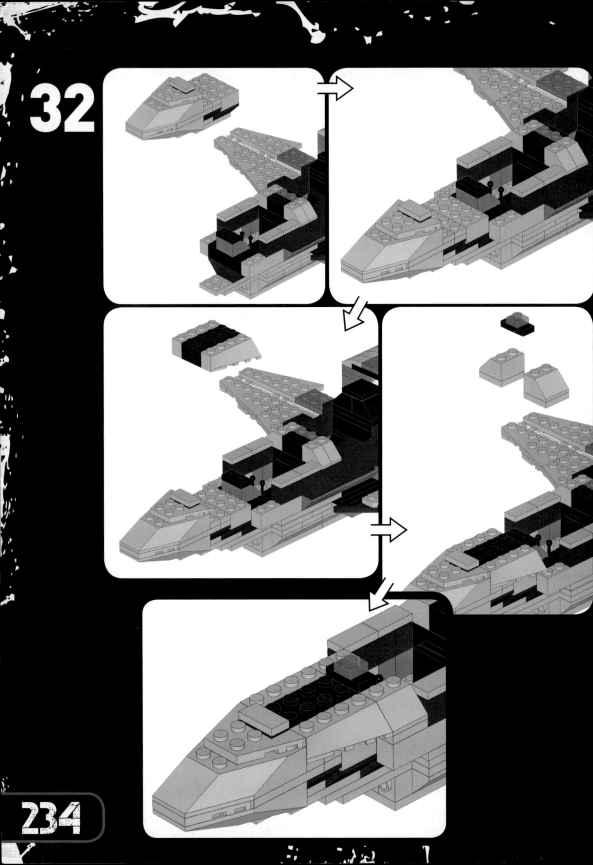

33

34

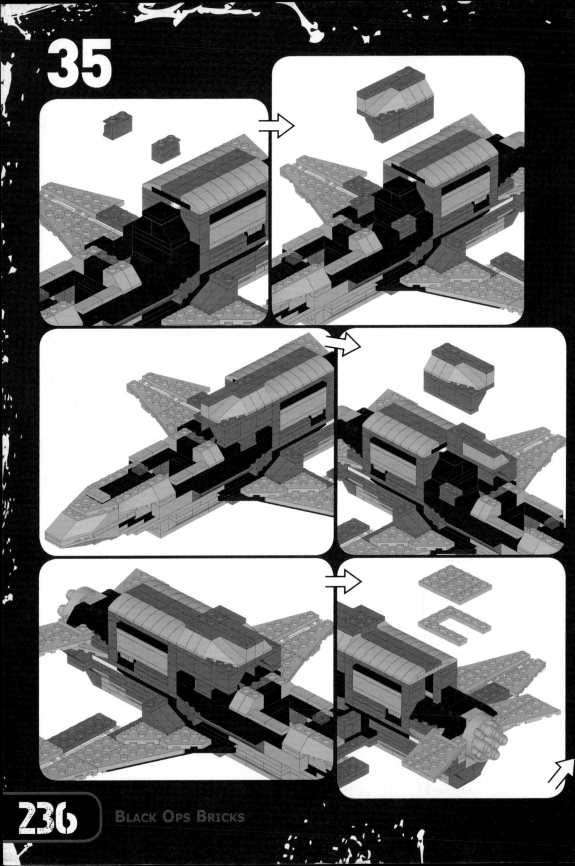

35

BLACK OPS BRICKS

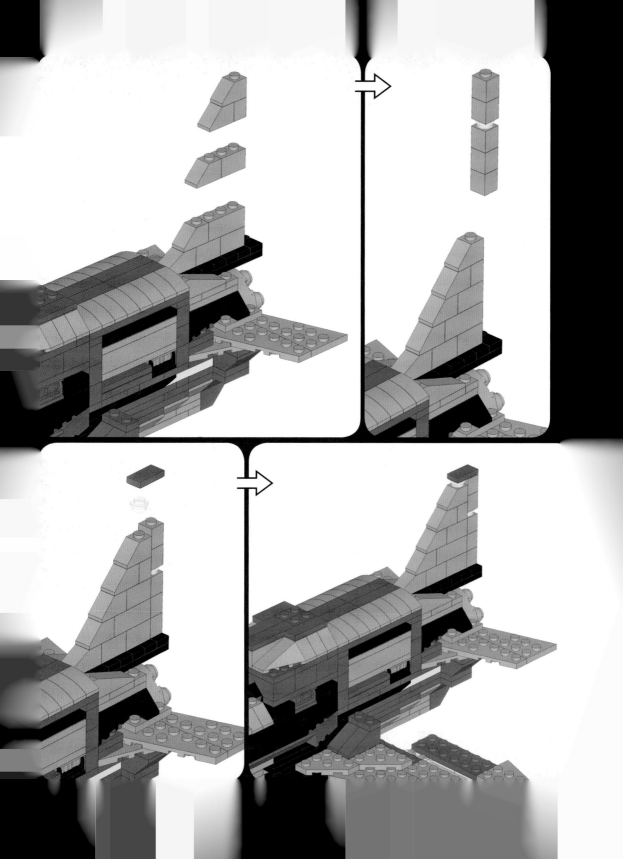

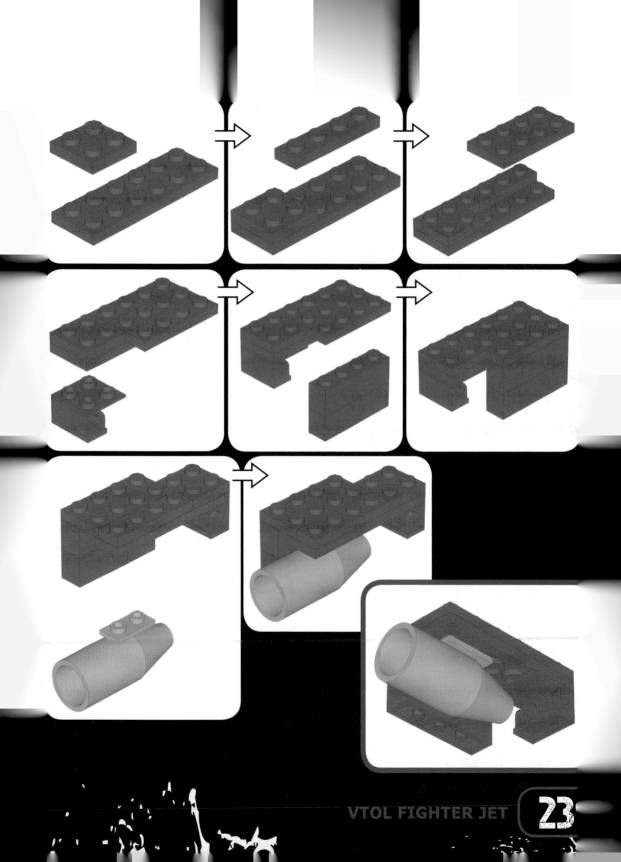

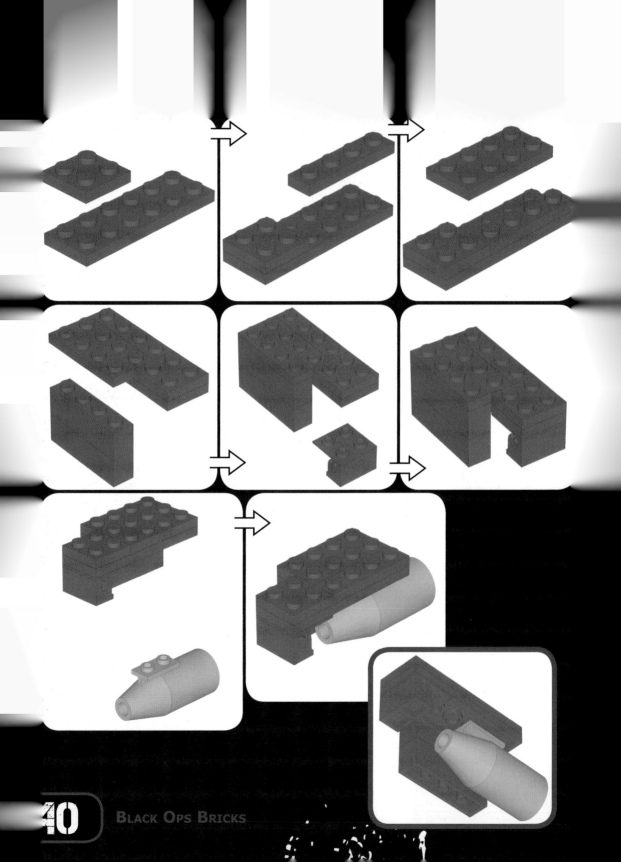

38

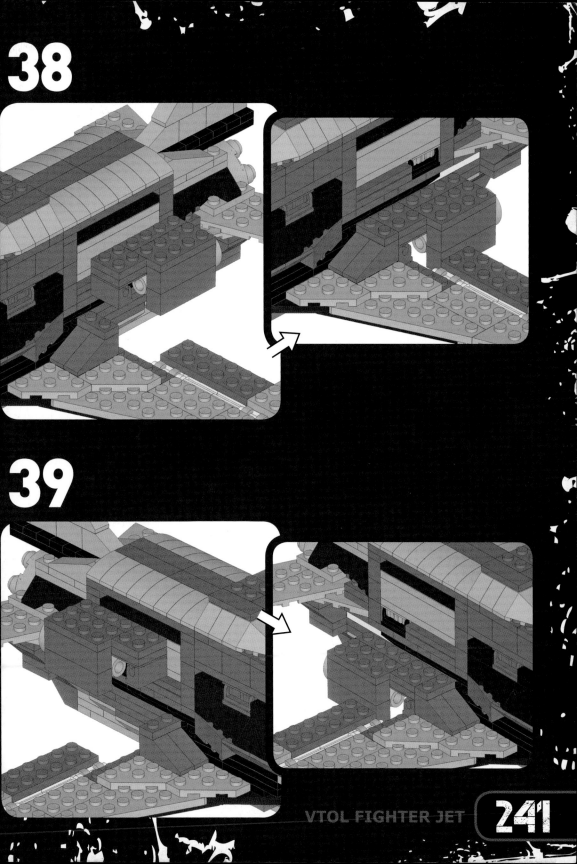

39

40

41

42

43

44

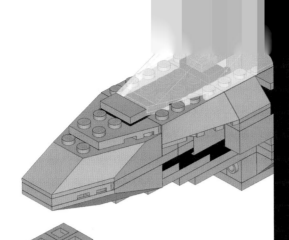

Done

DOWNLOAD THE DIGITAL FILES FOR EACH PROJECT AT:

BLACKOPSBRICKS.COM

Due to space restrictions and a desire to showcase a variety of projects, some of the larger builds have been left out. You can get a peek at the bonus models on the following pages. If you really want to dive in and try to tackle some of these more complex projects, download the digital files from the website.

You may also download the models and complete bill of materials for each of the projects in this book that have instructions. Download the models if you want a better look or if you want to modify any of these projects to suit your own needs.

EXCAVATOR
(EASILY MODIFIED FOR COMBAT OPS)

MOBILE MEDICAL CENTER
(AND COMMUNICATIONS RELAY)

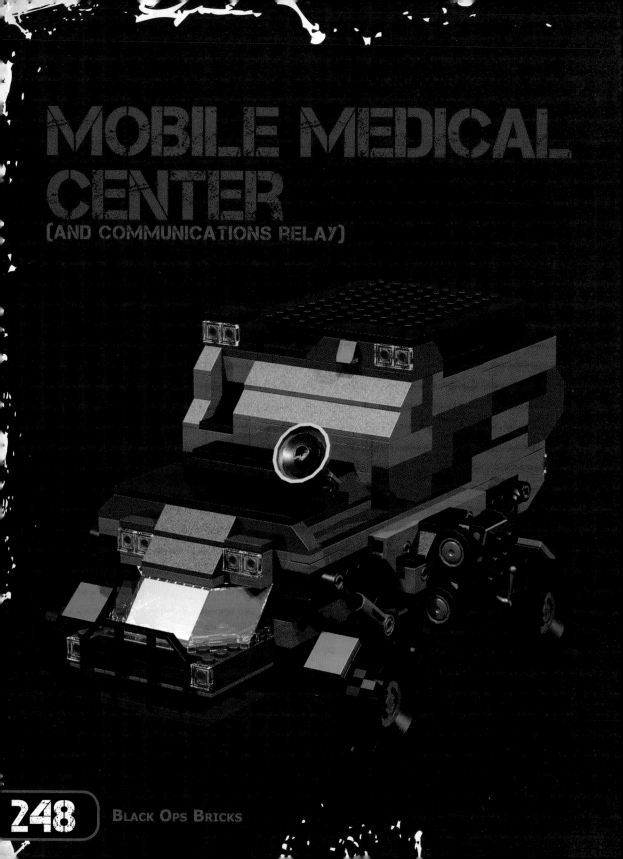

HOVERCRAFT
(TROOP AND VEHICLE TRANSPORT)

QUIK-LIFT
(SPEEDY, SHORT-TRIP, ON-BASE TRANSPORT)

BLACK OPS BRICKS

SCOUT CAR
(TWO-PERSON, LONG-RANGE, SURVEILLANCE CAR)

MECH SUIT
(ARTICULATE, FULLY-LOADED, BATTLE MACHINE)

SQUAD TANK
(LIGHT TANK USED FOR INFANTRY BACKUP)

COMMAND TANK
(HIGHLY SOPHISTICATED FULLY-ARMORED BATTLE STATION)

BLACK OPS BRICKS